A CONTRARIAN'S DICTIONARY:

2000 DAMNABLE DEFINITIONS

FOR THE YEAR 2000

By

Murray L. Bob

Contrarian Press

The Contrarian Press
571 Front Street
Jamestown, New York 14701

Designed by Darlene Lander

ISBN 0-9660154-0-1
Library of Congress Catalog Card Number 97-92494

Printed in the United States of America

First Edition
First Printing

Contrarian Press

TO THE READER:

In order of importance, my intention is, first, to make you smile inwardly if not outwardly and then to make you think. Not every definition will do both (some may not do either), but I'd like to believe that most readers will do at least one or the other, most times.

If you laugh out loud, it will be a bonus. If your life is changed, it will be a miracle - and I don 't believe in miracles. But, if some of the definitions cause you to say "Aha" or to view a thing from a fresh perspective, they will have done their job - which is to tickle or provoke. Some definitions are pure wordplay - nonsense, kidding around. So what? Shakespeare was the Pontiff of Pun. If he could do it, surely we pygmies can.

This is a book for sceptics, cynics, sinners, and deep-dyed contrarians. True believers read it at their own risk. Since the greatest joy contrarians can have is to communicate with others of their ilk, please let me know how you feel about the book and if you know of anyone else who might like to read it. There are many ways I can be reached, but I am contrary enough to prefer the old-fashioned way. Please write me. The address is: 571 Front Street, Jamestown, New York, 14701.

This is also the place to thank those who have put up with me and with the process that went into forming my strange thought processes or who helped with the manuscript: My mom and dad first (naturally); my wife, Renate, whose patience, good humor and kindness are boundless; Joseph Weber, the best thinker and writer I ever encountered, whose work is still largely unknown; and Catherine Way, who helped launch this ship. To issue the usual disclaimers: None of these worthies were or are responsible for anything written in these pages. Nevertheless, the book would not have appeared without them. But again, if you must blame someone, blame me entirely.

Oh, by the way, lest I forget: The marvelous illustrations are golden oldies, mostly by Wilhelm Busch, who also, unfortunately, remains largely unknown in the English-speaking world.

Enjoy!

Avant-Garde Art

A

Aardvark

AARDVARK:

Nobody ever died of it.

ABACUS:

Back-up if your computer crashes.

ABORTION:

If you don't trust a woman with a choice, how can you trust her with a baby?

ABSOLUTE TRUTHS:

What is sacred is the concept that nothing is sacred. What is infallible is the concept of fallibility. What is absolute is relativism. What is obsolete is absolutism.

ABSTINENCE:

Abstinence makes the heart grow fouler.

ABSURDITY:

There is no concept too absurd to become law.

ACCIDENT WAITING TO HAPPEN:

Death.

ACCOUNTABILITY:

The Mafiosi are the true Artists in Accountability: No paya da debt; No drawa da breath.

ACCURACY:

Never confuse accuracy with truth.

ACHIEVEMENT:

Our achievements eventually become our failures.

ACT OF GOD:

That used to be the excuse. Now the excuse is "the computer is down." Has It replaced God?

ACTING:

It's not so difficult being somebody else. It's being yourself that's tough.

ADDER:

It is hard to understand how this snake got its name, since it subtracts life.

ADMIRATION:

It's nice to be admired, as long as you don't share the feeling.

ADULATION:

As James Joyce said, "They would probably publish my collected pawn tickets."

ADULTERY:

Strictly for adults. Takes the monotony out of monogamy.

ADVERTISING:

People who claim they're not influenced by advertising believe their own advertising. Prostitutes sell their bodies. Admen sell their souls.

ADVICE:

The people who give the most advice are the ones who need it most.

ADVICE ON VICE:

Vice is nice. Those who crusade against it aren't.

ADVICE TO A FRIEND CONSIDERING RUNNING FOR PUBLIC OFFICE:

You have nothing to lose except your mind, your reputation, your family, your tranquillity, your honor, your fortune, and your privacy.

ADVICE TO THE AMBITIOUS:

1. Kick those below, flatter those above, and tailor your opinion to the prevailing pap. Power to the people - in power.
2. The best way to fit in is to be like everyone else - and complain of sameness.

Advice to the Ambitious

AFFIRMATIVE ACTION:

1. Just say no.
2. Was never a problem when it was called preferential treatment, i.e.; when the children of alumni and rich donors routinely made it into the best schools and jobs ahead of everyone else. It only became a problem when the same treatment was extended to people who had

been discriminated against in the past - Women, Afro-Americans, Hispanics, American Indians.

AFFLUENT SOCIETY:

Change the "a" to an "e" and you've got it right.

AGE OF AFFLUENCE:

When living sensibly was replaced by living sensuously.

AGE OF INNOCENCE:

Any female under five years of age and any unborn male.

AGE OF MIRACLES:

Ours is an age that believes in miracles, fully as much as the Middle Ages did - only the miracles we believe in are not spiritual, but technological. Being real doesn't make these miracles any the less phoney - only more dangerous.

AGEISM:

When I asked her why she invariably dated men 20 years her senior, she replied: "They're so grateful."

AGES OF MAN:

When I was young, I tried to change the world; when I was middle-aged, I tried to adapt to the world; now that I'm old, I try to ignore the world.

AGGRAVATION:

We only remedy our ills after we have aggravated them.

AGGRESSIVE PEOPLE:

You can always tell who the aggressive people are: They are the ones who accuse others of being aggressive.

AGING:

1. Outliving oneself.
2. The notion that things become clearer as you get older is absurd. You're at least as confused as you've ever been. What has changed is that now you don't expect answers.
3. It's nice to know you don't have long to go.
4. People don't get different as they get older, they become more like themselves.
5. You know you have aged when you have lost your lust.

Aging

3

AGING INSTITUTIONS:

By and large, aging institutions, like the Catholic Church, are run by aging staffs and younger institutions, like the computer industry, are run by younger staffs.

AGNOSTIC:

A God-fearing atheist.

AGREEMENT:

As Charles I said of Francis I: "My cousin and I are in complete agreement: We both want Milan."

AIR CONDITIONING:

Abolished the difference between inside and outside, the seasons and the climates, thereby enabling us to work 'round the clock everywhere around the world, and eliminating any possible excuse not to. This is progress?

AIRLINE TERMINALS:

The most boring places in the world. The only surprise in an airline terminal is the exorbitant price of the chewing gum. By contrast, 19th Century train stations were often architectural palaces. Still, the Airline Terminal is to the 20th Century what the Gothic Cathedral was to the 13th: Both, in their own way, reach heavenward. One by way of God; the other by way of Chicago.

ALARM:

We must never alarm people. That is why we never tell them the truth.

ALCHEMY:

The alchemists tried to convert all kinds of substances into Gold. Modern science has succeeded where they failed: It converts all kinds of knowledge into Cash Grants.

ALIENATION:

The country that gave us E.T.

ALTERNATIVE LIFE STYLES:

Dropping out; dropping dead.

ALTERNATIVE MEDICINE:

The other kind of quack medicine.

ALTRUISM:

1. It's a bear market for altruists these days: Try to give something away and people are immediately on their guard; try to sell it and they line up.
2. The difficulty is in knowing how to account for altruism. The argument from self-interest is that we are better off if we respect one another. The problem is that in many cases we may be better off yet, if we don't. Moreover, a person's *occasional* infraction is unlikely to hurt her or society appreciably. If altruism is not founded on self-interest, we are left with the old chestnut that virtue is its own reward. But what happens when it isn't? My contention is that altruism is like freckles: Existing in some people from birth and brought out by exposure to the sunlight of a warm environment.

AMBER WAVES OF GROAN:

What I love about this country is that it manages to combine the most advanced communications network with the most primitive social safety net, thereby ensuring that no matter how bad things get, your complaint will always be heard and nothing will be done about it.

AMBITION:

1. Compounded of equal parts of fear and greed.
2. So much effort, so little reward.
3. My ambition is to live without ambition.

AMERICA:

The Land of the Fee and the Home of the Rave.

THE AMERICAN DREAM:

Being paid more than you're worth.

ANAL SEX:

Asinine.

ANARCHY:

Anarchy is what we have. If you believe in the status quo, you are an anarchist.

ANATOMY:

Freud was wrong. Anatomy is no longer destiny, plastic surgery is.

ANIMAL LOVER:

There are two kinds of animal lovers: Those who love animals and those who love meat.

ANIMALS:

It is not that animals are less intelligent than people, it is that people define intelligence.

ANNUAL CHECK-UP:

Advisable on purely medical grounds - but only if your insurance pays for it. In the Czech Republic, these are called "Medical Czechs."

ANOMALY:

For the word "mystery," science substitutes the word "anomaly:" What's in anom?

ANSWERING MACHINES:

Their main purpose is to not answer.

ANTI-ACTIVIST:

Do nothing and you are already doing much - compared to the senseless scurrying about of the do-ers.

ANTI-SEMITISM:

For the Jew, his money can be as much a cause of as a protection against anti-Semitism.

ANXIETY:

The feeling that you will soon be in trouble. If you don't have this feeling, you are already in trouble.

APPEARANCES:

Appearances are deceiving - exactly as they are intended to be.

THE ARABIAN NIGHTS:

Phallic phables.

ARGUMENT:

Winning an argument doesn't mean you're in possession of the truth anymore than being in possession of the truth means you win the argument.

ARREST FOR VAGRANCY:

How we get even with people for having wronged them.

ARSONIST:

Believer in enlightenment.

ART:

1. Life is long, art is minimalist.
2. The function of art is not to cheer you up but to raise you up. There is a huge difference.
3. Doesn't explain, "merely suggests."
4. Enables us to see the familiar either for the first time or in a new way. Thus, art doesn't imitate, it makes things visible.

ART AND ADVERTISING:

Advertising is the "art" people *inhabit,* as opposed to the art they *visit* - in museums.

ART COLLECTING:

The acquisitive instinct masquerading as the aesthetic impulse.

ART CRITICISM:

The real art critics are the big collectors and dealers. They don't buy a painting because it is good, a painting is good because they buy it. Their purchase, if it involves a large enough sum, establishes the taste of the time - which is the taste not for art, but for money.

ARTIFICIAL INTELLIGENCE:

35 years ago the experts were predicting that artificial intelligence systems would do wonders in 10 years. They're still predicting they'll do wonders - in 10 years.

THE ARTISTIC PERSONALITY:

It is forgotten how recent the cult of the artist is. It began at the end of the 18th Century with *Sturm und Drang* and got going with Byron and Paganini. In medieval times, the names of artists and musicians were largely unknown or were made up much later by art historians. . .and the few ancient artists we do have the names of, we know next to nothing about. Our "loss" is art's gain.

ARTISTS:

Artists, like oysters, have to be irritated to produce pearls, which is why the worst times often produce the best artists.

ASCETIC:

He doesn't need much because he has a rich fantasy life.

ASPIRIN:

1. It's amazing what aspirin can cure. You should take aspirin even if nothing is wrong with you - you'll see, it will even cure that.
2. Why do the aspirin manufacturers have headaches? Now that it has been decided that aspirin helps prevent heart attack and colon cancer, they're having a problem trying to figure out how to charge more than when it was just for aches and pains.

ASSASSINATION:

Politicians are assassinated because it's sometimes the only way to shut them up.

ASTHMA:

There's no asthma like miasma.

ASTRONUTS:

It's not outer space we should be concerned with, but inner spaciness.

ASTROTURF:

The lawn of the future: You don't have to mow, water, weed, seed, feed, or spray it. Grass is for cows. Plastic is for people.

AT RISK:

If something or someone is not "at risk," you can't get funding for it. That's why so much is "at risk" these days. "Crisis" is the mother's milk of money.

ATOM BOMB:

Made in America; tested in Japan.

ATONEMENT:

Having children is the way we atone for what we did to our parents.

ATTENTION DEFICIT DISORDER:

Considering all the idiocies we're expected to pay attention to, this can't be too bad an affliction.

AUSTRALIA:

A vast continent subdued and settled by convicts. From the point of view of the Aborigines, of course, this was just another example of how Crime Marches On.

AUTHENTICITY:

The Existentialists tell us that in order to be authentic we have to choose. Every morning, I choose a different breakfast cereal, a different shirt, and a different pair of socks. That should do it.

AUTHOR, AUTHOR:

The successful author tickles the public's vanity by telling it what it already knows. The valuable author tells it what it doesn't know, doesn't want to hear, and has to make an effort to understand. Valuable authors are rarely successful in their own lifetimes which is one reason why they believe in immortality.

AUTHORSHIP:

Authorship has little to do with talent and much to do with celebrity. A murderer could sell his cancelled checks to a publisher.

AUTOMATION:

The machines get the jobs; the people get the sack.

THE AUTOMOBILE:

Wrecked our cities, fouled our air, and killed and maimed more people world-wide, year-in and year-out than any war in history except, possibly, World War II, which it will overtake and surpass in the 21st Century. The best population control device since war was invented.

AVAILABILITY:

Making something more available doesn't mean it will be used more. It may just make it more postponable.

AVANT-GARDE ART:

Commentary is necessary because confusion is evident.

AVOIDANCE THERAPY:

1. If you want to avoid making enemies, avoid making friends.
2. It's easy to avoid envy, jealousy, and spite - just don't get out of bed. Then, all you'll have to deal with are bedsores.

AWESOME:

Large football players; the Federal Deficit; Sumo wrestlers; Dolly Parton's boobs (pre-surgical).

9

Awesome

B

BABYTALK:

It is hard work raising babies. As far as I'm concerned, welfare mothers *are* fully employed.

BACK TO BASICS:

It depends on what you consider "basics" to be. If one looks dispassionately at history one could easily get the impression that people have always preferred fighting, fucking, and feasting to saving, slaving, and sowing.

BAD LUCK:

The best, all-purpose excuse.

BAD TIMES:

You have to be on a level with the times in which you live - even if it is a low level. Fortunately, as bad as the times are, we are just as bad, which is what makes them bearable.

BAD WORD?:

Why do people think that "shoot" is nice but "shit" isn't?

BALANCED BUDGET (How to Achieve):

1. Always put off 'till tomorrow, the payment of debts you incur today.
2. Make more expenses "off-budget."
3. Estimate future revenues higher. (Hey, it's only an estimate.)
4. A balanced budget is no remedy for an unbalanced social system.
5. The product of an unbalanced mind.
6. Just another gimmick to score political points..

BALLAST:

Every organization needs a few deadheads; a ship without ballast won't go straight.

BANGKOK:

Paradise Lust. Very popular with (s)expatriots in (s)exile and other tourists.

BANK:

I have very little *interest* in putting my money there...low interest produces no interest.

BAR MITZVAH BOY:

I used to believe problems could be solved. Then I grew up.

BAUHAUS:

The great deficiency of modern architecture is that it is devoid of whimsy: One misses grinning Gothic gargoyles - and boys. On the other hand, a Bauhaus dog-house would not be objectionable. One would, naturally, have to change the name of the style to Bow-wow haus.

BE:

"Be all that you can be." If we continue much longer trying to be all that we can be, we'll probably blow ourselves to kingdom come. Perhaps we should try being satisfied with just being. Heraclitus has had his day. It's time for a change to the changeless: Up with Parmenides.

BEAN:

Makes you fart, except for L.L. Bean - which makes you pay. Or Mr. Bean, who makes you laugh.

BEAUTY:

The problem with beauty is that I am not beautiful.

BED AND BREAKFAST:

Small room, small bed, small talk, and small portions - for small change. B & B's are very down-home. But the reason I go on vacation is to leave home.

BEFORE AND AFTER:

Often confused with cause and effect.

BEGGING:

Gelt for guilt - the beggar relieves you of your guilt. In exchange you give him gelt.

BEGINNING:

"Aller anfang ist schwer," said Goethe. (Every beginning is difficult.) That is because we agonize so much over precisely *where* to begin. Begin anywhere: The center is equidistant from any point on the circumference of the circle - and life is the circle whose center we seek.

BEING YOURSELF:

1. Eat, drink, and be Murray.
2. If you don't like the way you look, you buy a new face or figure; if you

don't like the way you think, you purchase a pill. The admonition "be yourself" has been replaced by the exhortation "buy yourself."

BELIEF:

1. The lazy person's substitute for thought.
2. I believe in disbelief.
3. Belief is the disease for which non-belief is the cure.
4. We need others to believe in us in order that we may believe in ourselves.

BELIEVING:

Comes from wanting to believe.

BENEFACTOR:

1. It's better to give than to receive - to give, you have to have; to get, you need to need.
2. Don't flatter the benefactor: She already feels superior.

BENIGN NEGLECT:

What you "do" when you don't want to make a mistake.

BEQUESTS:

1. Leave a good feeling in people's pockets.
2. The Remains of the Die.

BEST FRIEND:

The person you are *always* with; better get to know yourself better.

THE BEST THING:

The Best Thing would have been never to have been born at all. How many of us had that choice?

BETTERMENT:

Don't look for things to get better; look for better things.

BETWIXT AND BETWEEN:

What matters is what's between your ears and what's betwixt your legs.

BEYOND A REASONABLE DOUBT:

Nothing in life meets this standard: To reason is to doubt.

BIG BANG THEORY:

Married people who have been waiting for it all their lives consider it just a theory.

BIG BROTHER:

Everything about you is now in the computer: Big Brother is a data bank.

BIG CONFUSION:

Never confuse a big mouth with a big brain.

THE BIG PICTURE:

When someone tells you that you don't have "the big picture," your response should be that pictures are not valued by their size.

BIG TIPPER:

Bill Clinton promised us campaign reform; Al Gore promised us environmental progress; Hillary Clinton promised us health reform. Tipper Gore promised us she'd keep her mouth shut. Only Tipper has performed.

BILBUL:

If Clinton could Bill by the number of hours he spends *talking* about policy, he could singlehandedly wipe out the national debt. Surprising that his enemies don't call him Bull Clinton...yet...

THE BILL:

Always too high.

BILL AND HILLARY (The Arkansas Hillbillies):

Hillary said that when Bill was elected, the country would get two for the price of one. The problem with that is that by also having Hillary to pillory, there were now two *targets* for the price of one. Now we know why it wasn't done before - not for lack of ladies in the White House who wore the pants (*which* Reagan reigned was always a question, but which ruled - publicly - was not). If and when Al and Tipper make it, there won't be the same problem: Tipper ain't exactly a rocket scientist. In fact, between the two of them, there's too much bore for the media to Gore.

BIOTECHNOLOGY:

Biological evolution has been replaced by technological innovation; improvements in gadgets *are* improvements of the species.

BI-PARTISAN POLICY:

The police and the criminals are both against the decriminalization of drugs, since both benefit from the present policy.

BIRTH:

The worst (but fortunately the first) calamity.

BIRTH TRAUMA:

Up to now, children have not sued their parents for it. Wait...

BIZARRE:

If you can't be original, at least be bizarre. If you can't be bizarre, honesty is the best policy.

BLACK GHETTO:

The true extent of concern by the fortunate for the ghetto is limited to their worry about getting a bad tire or an overheated engine while driving through it with doors and windows locked and avoiding eye contact with the natives. The problem of the ghetto will never be solved until it is dissolved. The very existence of the ghetto makes it easy for those not in it, to avoid.

BLACK MAN'S BURDEN:

First oreos; now Orientials.

BLAME:

1. Somebody else.
2. The blamer.
3. Fundamentalists blame Satan for evil and the Left blames The Tri-Lateral Commission. When the Fundamentalists start to blame God and the Left starts to blame itself, we may have reason for hope.
4. Give people opportunities they don't take advantage of and they'll blame you.
5. Don't blame me for being happy.

BLANKET STATEMENT:

If I had my life to live over again, I'd go into the blanket business. Blankets have brought more bliss to more people than anything else.

BLUE RIBBON COMMITTEE:

Appointing a Blue Ribbon Committee to examine a problem is about as effective as extinguishing a raging fire by pissing on it.

BOASTS:

Boasts about one's ancestors are really boasts about oneself.

BOB PACKWOOD:

1. His crime was that he believed in congress more than he believed in Congress.
2. Packwood's expulsion from the Senate by colleagues who shared his priapic proclivities is reminiscent of the time politicians voted for Prohibition with flasks in their pockets.

BOBBITT:

What women do when they can't hack it.

BOB'S LAW:

Every computer system is sold on the basis of expected benefits and always falls below expectations.

BODY-BUILDING:

1. Inanity, insanity, but mostly vanity.
2. The body as billboard screaming: "Look at me, look at me."
3. Inflating the body to inflate the ego.

BONNIE AND CLYDE:

Love is a many-splattered thing.

BOOK BUSINESS:

Should really be called the Buck Business. Not so Gutenberg anymore.

BOOKS TO DOZE BY:

Some people can't get to sleep without reading. For them, books serve as sleeping pills without side-effects; what they seek are not page-turners, but page-tirers - few things being as effective at inducing sleep as a boring book. Publishers may be missing an opportunity if they promote stimulating but not soporific stuff. I can see the ad now: "This book is a real sleeper..."

BOOKWORM:

The glutton suffers from bulimia; the bookworm from booklemia.

BOOMS:

Booms are a bust: When things start getting better, people start acting worse.

BORDELLO BALLYHOO:

"We deflower in an hour."

BORE:

There are four ways a person can bore us:
1. By talking too much.
2. By talking too little.
3. By talking about something we're not interested in.
4. By talking about something we are interested in - instead of listening to us talk about it.

BORED:

1. People who claim they are never bored are boring. That's their secret: They keep from being bored by boring others.
2. At least when one is bored, one is not distracted.

BORN-AGAIN CHRISTIAN:

You would have thought once was enough.

BOSS:

1. One's superior; almost invariably one's inferior.
2. The boss is never wrong but often "misinterpreted."
3. The business is the ladder; the workers are the rungs. The boss gets to the top wronging the rungs

BOUNDARY:

The boundary between art and entertainment once blurred has now been erased.

BOX-OFFICE BOAST:

The pay's the thing.

BRAIN DEAD:

Thank God, the test of whether a person is brain dead does not involve the question of whether or not he *uses* his brain. If it did, we'd have to quadruple the number of cemeteries.

BRAINS:

1. When Beethoven's brother Karl sent a letter with the self-ascribed title, "Land-owner" after his signature, Beethoven responded with, "Brain-owner" attached to his name.
2. Q. Why is owning things so much more valued than owning brains?
   A. Because the people who do the valuing are brain-dead.

16

BRINKMANSHIP:

Edging up to the edge in hopes of making the other side edge back. If they don't, you do...unless, of course, you're stupid enough to call your own bluff. An edgy affair, at best.

BRUTE FARCE:

Mussolini.

BUDDHA:

To be freed of need is to be wanting in want. But the absence of desire is death.

BUDGET PROJECTIONS:

Classified by librarians under the subject-heading, "Fairy-tales, Myths, and Legends."

BUG:

Once an insect, now a hidden recorder. One bites, the other transcribes. In either case, it's a sting operation.

BULLSHIT:

The art form our age excels in.

BUNGEE JUMPING:

When death-defying turns into death-denying. We could do with less derring-do and more daring don't.

BUOYANCY:

Gaite, courage, fierté should be our watchwords.

BUREAUCRACY:

The biggest bureaucracy is the one least criticized - the military; the most useless bureaucracy is actually worshipped - the church. The smallest bureaucracy, one that may even, on rare occasions, do some good is the least respected - welfare. It isn't how well a bureaucracy serves that matters, but whom it serves. We live in a time when the only kind of serving that is really understood is self-serving.

BUSINESS LETTER:

The criticism is always the same: "It's too long. They never read more than one page." The perfect business letter fits on the back of a postage stamp and consists of one word: "Buy."

BUSINESS RELIGION:

In America, business is a religion and religion is a business: In one case, you're selling goods; in the other case, good feelings.

BUSINESSMAN:

The Very Highest Type of Humanity. *The* Latter-Day Saint. Always characterized by Vision, Generosity, and an uncanny ability to avoid paying taxes, while denouncing government spending and the Federal Deficit and simultaneously scrounging subsidies, grabbing government contracts and overcharging the feds as much as possible.

BUYERS AND SELLERS:

As buyers, we seek truth; as sellers, we fabricate falsehoods.

C

CALL WAITING:

The end of civilized conversation as we know it.

CAMPAIGN PROMISES:

1. Why are campaign promises like farts? Both consist of hot air and neither has any lasting effect.
2. Campaign promises are about as likely to be honored as your child's promise to repay what you loaned him.

"CAN DO" ATTITUDE:

1. Especially useful if you are constipated.
2. People who "get a lot done" are probably wasting their lives.

CANCER:

A growth industry.

CANDIDATE SELECTION:

We'd do better picking names out of a hat.

CANINE CANON:

I always root for the underdog; I always try to be top dog.

CANNIBALISM:

1. Vastly underrated both as a source of protein and as a method of population control. In Fiji, the cannibals were said not to like the taste of people who had smoked. Thus, a re-introduction of cannibalism

might encourage smoking and be of assistance to struggling tobacco companies.

2. One man's meat is another man.

3. You'd rather be eaten by worms?

CAN'T DO ATTITUDE:

When there's nothing you can do, do nothing...Well, you could try thinking.

CAPITAL PUNISHMENT:

1. How come they never punish the real criminals in this country - the ones who work at the Capitol?

2. There are days when I think that there's nothing wrong with capital punishment that a change of victims wouldn't remedy.

3. An article of faith for those who believe in The Nine Commandments.

CAPITALISM:

1. A fatal disease with no known cure.

2. The most successful social system in the history of the world. Nothing fails like success.

3. Marx might have called it entremanureship. Considering most of *what* gets produced, it could also be called crapitalism.

4. Capitalism offers a comfortable position to every person of talent or energy who conforms, and every such person speaks of capitalism's "good side."

5. You can't regulate it, you have to replace it.

CARD-PLAYING:

The tomb of time.

CARE:

What do women want? To take care of things. What do men want? To be taken care of.

CAREER ADVANCEMENT:

Based less on what you know than whom you blow.

CAREER CHOICES:

There are many ways of making a living. Unfortunately, few of them constitute living.

CAREER COUNSELING:

1. Religion has always offered steady employment. You won't make quite as much money as the great villains who own the world, but you need

never starve. There are always more than enough suckers and sinners whose consciences can be prickled, pickled, tickled, and tormented.
2. If you don't like to obey, command; if you don't like to command, obey. If you don't like either, marry money.

CARING:

The idea is to care about things - not to carry on about them.

CASTLE TOURS:

At least they don't make you Disney.

CATHOLICISM:

Historically, Catholicism offered us saints and Protestantism offered us savings.

CELEBRITY:

1. The surest way to achieve celebrity is to murder one.
2. Celebrity is a certain sign of mendacity, mediocrity, or vulgarity. The rare exceptions are strictly temporary.
3. To be noticed, be outrageous.

CEMETERIES:

1. Just about the only places left where they don't sell pizza.
2. Cemeteries are wasted on the dead. It's the living who need peace and quiet.

CENSORSHIP:

1. Might better be called senseless-ship: There's no way to control information; what people won't get one way they'll get another. Attempts at censorship make the object censored more desirable, thereby raising its price.
2. Self-censorship is more dangerous than censorship because it is covert, unaccountable, preemptive, unchallengeable and because what is not produced cannot be retrieved.
3. It's Nazi-easy to know what to do when freedom of expression threatens freedom of expression.

CENSUS:

Those that don't get counted, don't exist. Makes sense-us, doesn't it?

CEO:

1. Someone who hires people to make his mistakes for him and then fires them because they did their jobs.
2. Incomprehension obscured by soaring salary.

CEO/BOARD RELATIONSHIP:

If you don't control the Board, the Board controls you.

C'EST LA WOE:

To complain is human; to whine divine.

CHALLENGE:

Brings out the beast in you.

CHANGE:

1. Unimportant things change; important things don't.
2. From Babbitt to Bobbitt.
3. Political ideas are changed like neckties: Political realities are changed like glaciers.
4. We have substituted change for difference.

CHANGE AGENT:

Everyone likes the idea of change; few like actual change. Everyone thinks others should change, but hates it when others think they should change.

CHANNELING:

Politics has exhausted its possibilities and been replaced by entertainment: You don't change the world, you change the channel.

CHAOS THEORY:

One thing you can say about Chaos Theory is that it's creating a lot of chaos. We needed that. As for fractals: They're responsible for only a fractal of the confusion you see everywhere. The rest is due to the blurring of the sexes.

CHARACTER ASSASSINATION:

They don't put you in jail for this form of assassination, so it is the preferred weapon of Cowards, Columnists, and Congresspersons. Congress is protected by immunity, the columnists by laughable libel laws, and cowards by the use of untraceable rumors.

CHARISMA:

All truly great leaders (and misleaders) have this indefinable quality which is best described by what it does, rather than by what it is. Charismatics feed people's desperate hunger for someone or something to believe in. What they feed it with is a judicious mixture of fact, fad, and fancy.

CHARITY:

1. Giving money to charities with billion dollar endowments is like washing ducks.
2. You may empathize with the dispossessed, but if you are not one of them, it's all very abstract. And even if you *were* one of them, the memory grows weak and plays tricks: You start to think that just because *you* could get out of the misery, they should be able to, conveniently overlooking the cultural and the material advantages you started life with. Charity is fundamentally inadequate. People need to *be* equal, not just to be "treated" as equal.

THE CHARLATAN:

His tongue is his tool.

CHASTITY:

1. The problem with it is that a starving person is not likely to spend much time poring over the menu. In a word, a too prolonged chastity leads to "any port in a storm."
2. Ignorance as virtue.

CHECKS AND BALANCES:

Greatest system ever invented to insure gridlock.

CHEEK:

If you turn the other cheek often enough, you won't be able to sit down.

CHEEKY:

College students who moon are said to be cheeky.

CHILD ABUSE:

When the child abuses the parent (Hah!).

Cheeky

CHILDHOOD:

Once considered a golden age, it is now thought to be a period of great abuse, especially by parents and close relatives. If you have pleasant memories of childhood you are said to be repressing the truth. If you have painful memories, you are thought to need help "to work through them." Fortunately, wise and (and expensive) counsellors are available to lighten your load of guilt and gelt. And if you don't have the money, insurance will pay for it. Amazing how the increase in diseases correlates with the increase in coverage.

CHILDREN:

Children

1. Children today get everything they want. That is the problem. They are deprived of deprivation. The consequence: Children have no fantasy life: They no longer need one. Between prefabricated images that replace imagination and Instant Gratification, which does away with the need for anticipation and hope, what they end up with is - everything. And that is nothing.
2. Cute, but think what they'll be like when they grow up.

CHILDREN'S TELEVISION:

Since people can only buy 'till they die, it's important to start them shopping early.

CHINA:

You don't need statistics: One concentration camp is enough.

CHINA'S DEMOCRATIC REFORMS:

Stalin's Constitution of 1936 also promised basic rights to everyone.

CHINA'S FUTURE:

When a car's in every garage, fresh air'll be a mirage.

CHINESE POPULATION CONTROL EXPERT:

Daughter aborter.

CHIROPRACTIC:

A bang on the back by a quack to make a quick buck from a schmuck.

CHIROPRACTORS:

What astrologers are to astronomers, chiropractors are to M.D.'s.

CHOICE:

1. Pay now or pay later.
2. The choice is not between good or evil, the choice is between good *and* evil or nothing at all.

CHOICE ADVICE:

Never offer a choice unless you don't really care which choice is made.

CHOICES:

1. Fortunately, in this country we don't have to choose between being rich and being powerful.
2. One can be either an atheist or an atavist.
3. A life can have rhyme or it can have reason. It rarely has both.

CHRISTIAN CONSERVATIVES:

They don't seem to mind if governments intrude in the personal lives of people, as long as governments don't intrude on people's ability to make money. Christian Conservatives want to legislate morality in the bedroom, not in the boardroom.

CHRISTIANITY:

Changing bread and wine into flesh and blood was nothing compared to Christianity's real achievement: Changing sex into sin.

CHRISTMAS CADS:

People who send family newsletters at Christmas time...as though anyone cares...

CHUNNEL:

Constructed because they saw the loot at the end of the tunnel.

CHURCH ATTENDANCE:

What some people do Sunday mornings before they have a really wrenching religious experience - watching professional football.

CHURCHES:

What is nice about a big, quiet, empty, old church is that it is big, quiet, empty and old. Just like God.

CHURNING:

The broker's commissions multiply as the investor's dough divides.

CIGARETTE ADS:

When First Amendment rights became First Amendment wrongs.

CIRCULAR REASONING:

1. The only kind there is. If it's not circular, it's not reasoning.
2. Going around in circles is one way to deepen your experience.

CIRCUMSTANTIAL EVIDENCE:

1. Only persuasive in the case of poor people since poverty is evidence of felony.
2. We don't know what we're capable of until we're tested - not by tests, but by circumstance.

CIVICS 1:

This is not a democracy; it's a plutocracy. It's not the people who rule; money rules.

CIVIL RIGHTS:

Why is it that so many people who talk about Civil Rights are neither?

CIVIL SERVANT:

1. Mostly servile; rarely civil.
2. Won't trade a comfortable present for a glorious future.

CIVIL SERVICE PROMOTION:

Upward slowbility.

CIVILIAN CONTROL OF THE MILITARY:

The reason that the military will never take over the U.S. Government is that it does not need to since it is not accountable to the government. It is the military that really decides its own budget and the actual use of the money it receives. It does not even have to tell Congress what all its operations are - although it is Congress that votes its funds. Civilian control of the military amounts to about as much as majority control of Congress.

CLARITY:

If the criterion of clarity is that a thing always be *immediately* intelligible to *everyone* then writing has been replaced by advertising.

CLASS-STRUGGLE UPDATED:

The class struggle has been replaced by the ass struggle The world is now divided between those who kick ass and those who kiss ass.

CLEAN AIR ACT:

It is an act: We haven't had clean air since we took over from the Indians.

CLEAVAGE:

The Parton of the ways.

25

CLIENT GOLF:

You need balls to play. But you've got to let the client play with them.

CLINTON:

1. Give the devil his due. Clinton has managed to lower the moral tone, which had become insufferable.
2. Strong on facts, weak on truth.
3. Survival of the flabbiest.
4. The attitude of gratitude comes naturally. Clinton just wants to be loved - which is why he keeps running for office - before, during, and after election.
5. What does Clinton stand for? He stands for election - what else?
6. A Republican disguised as a Democrat.

CLINTON'S ACHIEVEMENTS (First Term):

Poor people got less, rich people got more. Forget party labels, Clinton is the man best able to realize the Reagan-Bush agenda.

CLIO:

What is history? The record of errors past. We study it to avoid making the same mistakes, thereby giving ourselves an opportunity to make new mistakes. That doesn't make the study of history useless: The buoys and beacons anchored where ships were wrecked yesterday help us navigate today.

CNN HEADLINE NEWS:

Half truths for half-wits.

COCA COLA:

Originally sold as a headache cure, Coca Cola was re-invented as a mass beverage. Asa Candler, who bought the patent from a pharmacist, reasoned that "the chronic sufferer from headaches may have but one a week. Many persons have only one a year. There was one dreadful malady, though, that everybody...suffered from daily...which during six or eight months of the year would be treated and relieved, only to develop again within less than an hour. That malady was thirst."

COCKROACHES:

Has anyone ever listened to their side of the story?

COERCION:

1. I call it coercion when unpleasant people are pleasant, and you are forced to be pleasant in return.
2. Coercion is not the solution; it is the problem.

COFFEE:

The introduction of coffee sobered Europe after a centuries-long debauch during which people of all classes wallowed in wine and beer. Coffee was as necessary to the rise of capitalism as the Protestant Reformation. Both were needed if a "work ethic" was to take hold.

COFFEE GROUNDS:

Has beans.

COFFIN:

A hotel without a wake-up call.

COFFIN NAILS:

Q. Should advertisements for cigarettes be banned?
A. No. It is vital to preserve the principle of free expression.
Q. What, then, do we do to discourage smoking?
A. Cigarette ads should be allowed but only on the backs of tombstones.

COJONES:

The University of Chicago denied the Queen of England an Honorary Doctorate because she had not contributed to scholarship.

COLD WAR:

We had World War I. Then we had World War II. After that we had Cold War I. Then Communisim collapsed. Now we have Cold War II - being waged by Judeo-Christian Civilization against Islam or, if you prefer, by the developed world against the underdeveloped. The "enemy" keeps changing, but war remains. So, the real issue is not War or Peace, but Hot or Cold.

COLLAPSE OF COMMUNISM:

From repression to corruption.

COLOURIZATION:

The best way to make old black and white movies colourless is to colorize them - or should we say colonize them?

COLUMNIST:

The nice thing about being a newspaper columnist is that you can offer an opinion about everything, without having a clue about anything.

COMEDY:

All comedy is based on mistakes, but not all mistakes are comic.

COMEDY CENTRAL:

Only humor should be taken seriously. Everything else is a joke.

COMING OUT OF THE CLOSET:

1. All the rage. But what of the fun to be had in the closet - that extra little frisson of pleasure one got from doing what one shouldn't do and getting away with it? And what about the privacy, warmth, and shelter of the closet? Today, if you have it, you're supposed to flaunt it - on Geraldo or Sally Jessie Raphael. Coming out of the closet may prove you have courage or it may prove you are a fool. The only thing it proves with certainty is that you're an exhibitionist.
2. People may come out of the closet, but that does not mean that the closet comes out of them. *Everyone* still hides some things, still wears a mask more often than not, and returns to the closet time and again.

COMMITMENT:

To be committed to non-commitment is a form of commitment.

COMMITTEES:

1. Where forms are followed and substance is ignored.
2. Where more attention is paid to the representation of vested interests than to the interest of majority representation.

COMMON SENSE:

In senseless world, making sense may no longer make sense.

COMMUTER AIRLINES:

1. Fly and die.
2. America's Aeroflot.

COMPASSION:

What about compassion for the people who have to put up with compassionate people? Have you actually lived with someone who makes it a daily practice to pick-up stray animals, people, or causes?

COMPENSATION:

The worse the job, the worse the compensation; the better the job, the better the compensation. Given these circumstances, the term, "compensation" has little meaning.

COMPLAINING:

1. Such a comfort.
2. Stop complaining already, there's much worse to come.

3. Women complain more than men, which is why they live longer.
4. Why is it that everyone complains of lack of money, but no one complains of lack of sense?

COMPLICATION:

The most complicated thing I know is trying to make things simple.

COMPOSITION:

In Mozart's case we call it composing; in Cage's case, we call it decomposing.

COMPROMISE:

1. Avoiding choice.
2. The way you make your living is the way you compromise yourself.

COMPUTER:

An upwardly-mobile typewriter.

COMPUTER COMMUNICANT:

Never alone; ever alone.

COMPUTER CRASH:

When the computer crashes, there is frustration and irritation, but also a frisson of gratification. Is this because at a certain level we see the computer as competitor, enemy, heir - a threat to our jobs, our lives and perhaps ultimately to our superior position as a species? The Oedipus Complex of the 21st Century may not involve the urge to kill the father (by then, who will even know his identity?) but to kill the computer.

COMPUTER CRAZE:

In a loveless world, at least we have our computers.

COMPUTER GEIST:

With computers man has finally succeeded in creating ghosts: You communicate with people you don't see, hear, smell, touch, or taste.

COMPUTER LITERACY:

1. Ranks right up there with lawnmower literacy.
2. Nowadays the computers are literate, but the people aren't. They say you can't get a job unless you know computers, but it seems that the computers are getting the jobs.

COMPUTER NERD:

Gear queer.

COMPUTER SYSTEMS:

The Cold War being over, something had to take the place of cannons to keep the economy going. . .and lo, there were computers.

COMPUTERS:

Help people do things they could not do before...which doesn't mean they're worth doing or will be done. Unproven claims about what computers will do for you are as abundant as pollen in September.

COMPUTHINK:

The question is not whether computers can think, but whether people can.

CON ARTISTS:

Con artists are the first to be conned.

CONDOMS:

If they would put condoms on cigarettes instead of penises, we might be able to enjoy both sex *and* smoking.

CONFERENCE:

Vacation on company time. The best way to enjoy it is to arrive sober, leave sober, and be drunk the entire time between.

CONFESSION:

It is no longer fashionable to confess the truth, which is usually very boring. It is far more fun to confess to terrible things that never happened.

CONFIDENTIAL:

To tell someone something "in confidence" is to assure their undivided attention. To ask them to "keep it in confidence" is to ask of them what you were unable to ask of yourself: The impossible.

CONFLICT RESOLUTION:

I prefer resolute conflict (without bloodshed) to conflict resolution (without principle).

CONNECTIVITY:

The more connected we are electronically, the less connected we are humanly.

CONSENSUS:

1. When everyone agrees to the wrong thing.
2. Something everyone lauds, but no one practices.
3. The process of abandoning all beliefs, principles, and values.
4. Coerced conformity.
5. Dictatorship masquerading as democracy: Is not dissensus as important as consensus?

CONSENTING ADULTS:

If they were *really* adult, they probably wouldn't.

CONSERVATION:

Only takes place when the chance to squeeze every last penny out of nearly extinct species or a nearly desertified place has disappeared. Clearly, conservation suffers from constipation.

CONSERVATIVE JUDGEMENT ON THE 20TH CENTURY:

We have travelled from a time when nothing was permitted to a time when everything is perverted.

CONSERVATIVES:

Snobs are not all conservatives, but all conservatives are snobs.

CONSISTENCY:

If you reflect on how often you have changed your mind, you will never again be adamant.

CONSOLATION:

1. There is always the consolation that there is none.
2. Not many Afro-Americans leapt to their deaths during The Great Depression. It's hard to commit suicide jumping out of a basement.

CONSPIRACY THEORY:

Sensible people don't believe in conspiracies, which is why crazy people get away with them.

CONSTIPATION:

1. When tush comes to shove.
2. The riddle of the Sphinx.

Constipation

CONSTRUCTIVE CRITICISM:

Criticism that "merely" smashes icons and shatters harmful illusions *is* good in itself. The so-called constructive critic would replace one idol by another that he is probably peddling for personal profit.

CONSULT:

Considering how uninformed and ill-informed most people are, why would you want to?

CONSULTANT:

When something is obvious, necessary and unpopular, you never do it - you hire a consultant to recommend it. N.B. Never hire a consultant without first telling him what conclusion you want his unbiased study to arrive at. Also, beware of the consultant who, tired of hustling contracts, is looking for a steady job: He may want yours.

CONSULTANT REPORTS:

Consultant

Fairytales for grown-ups.

CONSUMER REPORTS:

Usually, the "Best Buy" is don't buy.

CONSUMER SOCIETY:

1. If the consumer is king, then advertising must be King Kong.
2. You think you will have a ball at the mall, but you will be mauled: Things purchased will, over time, cost twice the price and be half as useful as you imagined.

CONTAINMENT:

Containment has replaced contentment, both as policy and ideal: Contained wars, depressions, and rage characterize the times.

CONTENTMENT:

Little white powders, pills, and lies lighten life.

CONTRADICTION:

I may contradict myself, but I don't contradict the truth which is itself contradictory.

CONTRADICTIONARIES:

Down with dictionaries! We are enslaved by definitions. Life is brimful of contradictions. What we need are CONTRADICTIONaries.

CONTRARIETIES:

A man is known by the company he avoids. A penny saved is useless. Better late than early. Do what I say, not what you think. Half a loaf is a lot to eat at one sitting. A snitch in time stops crime. Honesty is the worst policy.

CONTRIBUTING TO THE TWO POLITICAL PARTIES:

Watering last year's crop.

CONTRIBUTION:

They also contribute who, by their excesses, help the present exhaust itself.

CONTROL:

1. Being "in control" means that you are in control of the appearance that you are in control.
2. When the goal is control, the result is anarchy.

CONVENIENCE

In order to encourage shopping, we made parking convenient. Now, people shop *because* parking is free, nearby, available, safe, covered, etc. Thus, the means come to determine the ends. People will do things and go places because they are handy not because they need or want to. Everything has become so quick and easy, we no longer inquire whether it is worthwhile...and even if it's expensive, it "costs less than it used to," which is supposed to make it "cheap"...or "someone else (third party payment) is paying for it"...which makes it *seem* cheap...or we can buy it on credit. Convenience is killing us - we have made a god of it, and it has made slaves of us - which is what gods alway end up doing.

CONVENIENT TRUTH:

Telling the truth is easier than lying, which is often why people tell the truth.

CONVENTIONAL MORALITY:

Conventional morality is an ass that needs to be flayed, a set of rules that needs to be flaunted, evaded, eluded, and denuded. Adherence to it is, however, convenient, hence its "popularity."

CONVERSATION:

There's no way to have a real conversation if the people you're having it with aren't real.

Conversation

CONVICTIONS:

1. If you want to know which persons have convictions, count their enemies: More convictions, more enemies.
2. Fossilized thoughts.
3. It is easier to abandon convictions then it is to abandon the tendency to acquire them.

COOPERATION:

When neighbors get together to gang up on an outsider.

COPIES:

We spend our energy making copies ever closer to the real thing, thereby getting further from the real thing. Copies reproduce the result, not the history. They provide product, not process; text, not context.

COPING:

Planning is what we think; coping is what we do.

COPING WITH DISASTER:

The best way to cope with one disaster is to court another.

COPPER DEFICIENCY:

More policemen are needed.

CORDLESS PHONES:

Invisible chains.

CORN FLAKES:

There are 200 "different" breakfast cereals (all pretty much the same) only 10% of the cost of any of which is for the ingredients. The answer to the question, "What's in a name?" is: Just about everything. The package *is* the product.

CORRESPONDENCE SCHOOL:

Home study drop-out rates exceed 60% - which proves that there's no correspondence between reality and the claims of correspondence schools.

CORRUPTION:

Its defenders say that corruption is not characteristic of the system; its opponents say it is the system.

COUNTRY AND WESTERN:

Muzhik music.

COURAGE:

Courage is admirable, but let's not forget some of the things that require it: Lying, stealing, and murder.

COURT BACKLOGS:

If judges were paid by the decision instead of being on salary, there'd be a big dent made in the pile-up of cases pending trial.

COVER-UP:

From the inside, everything is a mess. Cover-up.

COWARD:

1. A person who inflicts no harm on others in the hope that by such discretion he will avoid giving others a pretext to harm him. Unhappily, many people need no pretext. At least the coward tries to stay out of trouble; what are needed now are crowds of cowards.
2. To be cowardly may be as much a matter of choice as to be brave. Neither choice is appropriate for every occasion.

COWARDLY THOUGHT:

Cowards are generally brighter than heroes.

COWS:

Hamburgers on the hoof. But can they ketchup?

Cows

CRAP:

In the final analysis, everything is crap, but crap isn't everything.

CRAZY:

1. Everybody's crazy. Some people think they're not crazy. They're really crazy.
2. Everybody has a right to be crazy, but they don't have a right to make others crazy.

CREATIONISM:

I believe in creationism: Man created God.

CREATIONISM IN THE CONSUMER SOCIETY:

In the beginning was the word. And the word was "Buy."

CREDIT:

1. Yourself.
2. There is no doctrine or dogma so stupid that masses of people won't be found to credit it.

CREME DE LA CREME:

The rich man cries when he is robbed, while the poor man thinks: "Who is he to complain? What has he ever done except rob?"

D

DAMAGE CONTROL:

Making molehills out of mountains.

DANGER:

People who "always know their own mind" and "never suffer from doubt" are dangerous.

THE DARK AGES:

1. Before electricity.
2. You say that I am a pessimist because I call the period we are in "The Dark Ages." Not so: The night is long, but it does not last forever.

DAY-DREAMING:

I have no time to do things; I'm much too busy day-dreaming. In general, people ought to do less. A lot of them ought to do nothing.

DAYLIGHT SAVING TIME:

Whenever anyone objects to the encroachments of what is euphemistically termed "progress," someone else is sure to say, "But, you can't turn back the clock." Why not? We do it every year in order to save daylight. Why can't we do it to save wetlands, species, lives?

DAYTIME TELEVISION:

Soap Oprah.

DEAD-END:

Let us frankly recognize that we are fresh out of ideas of how to save the world or ourselves. So what? We are, after all, not dead...merely at a dead-end. Dead-ends exist and have existed before...Life goes on...

DEATH:

1. Finally: Some peace and quiet.
2. A lot of people have died trying to avoid it.
3. How else would we get rid of serial killers, tyrants, and rock stars?
4. The only thing left that you can count on. Don't let them take it away.
5. The possibility of impossibility; thus, the ultimate possibility.
6. A minor incident that should be ignored.

DEATH AT AN EARLY AGE:

One thing you can say for it: It saves a lot of time.

DEATH WISH:

The advantage of death over life is that in the case of life, you can only wish for it to be long; in the case of death, you *know* it will be long.

DEATH WITH DIGNITY:

Another empty phrase. We don't talk of "sex with dignity" or "urination with dignity." Death is natural, why does it need to be dignified as well? The phrase is the product of a civilization which still hides from the natural, preferring to cover it with words.

DEBT:

The national debt need not concern us. After all, we owe it to ourselves (only 20% of the national debt is owned by foreign interests, and that percentage is *lower* that it was), and we are famously forgiving of our own excesses. It is not too surprising that worry about the debt is vastly over-blown when we consider that the owners of the debt own the media along with everything else. The way you deal with debt is the way you deal with post-coital triste: Roll-over.

DECADES OF DECADENCE:

What the '60's were for the Left, the '90's are for the Right.

DECENCY:

You can be decent or you can be rich, but it's hard to be both.

DECEPTION:

1. If deception isn't natural, how come animals use camouflage?
2. We deceive others in order to deceive ourselves.
3. People who do not succeed in deceiving others often succeed in deceiving themselves that they failed because they were too honest.

DECISION THEORY:

The theory that you make your own decisions.

DECLINE:

Pessimism fears a decline; optimism is a decline.

DECLINE AND FALL OF WESTERN CIVILIZATION:

At the beginning of this century America created parks. At the end of this century, it creates golf courses.

DEER DROPPINGS:

Best microwaved and served piping hot on a bed of lettuce.

DEFAMED:

What De Rich and De Famous ought to be. Would that they could be De Fanged as well.

DEFICITS:

Keynes was right - deficits are not the problem, they're the solution.

DEFINITION:

1. The way you define your terms is the way you define your times.
2. Be careful how you define your problems or you may be forced to deal with them.
3. To define is to confine.

DEGREE:

You get a degree in order to speak impressively and write incomprehensibly.

DELEGATION:

Some bosses don't delegate enough and some delegate too much. The first don't trust anyone else; the second don't trust themselves.

DELUSION:

Of the many delusions that rule and ruin our lives, the greatest may be the notion that we *must* endure ills the least effort might remedy.

DEMOCRACY:

1. People just can't spell anymore: Should be "dumbocracy."
2. Invoked everywhere; found nowhere.

DEMOCRATIC REFORM IN RUSSIA:

Much thunder; little rain. Much lightning; little light.

DEMOCRATS:

Hypocrites are not all Democrats, but all Democrats are hypocrites.

DEN OF THIEVES:

Post-industrial society.

DENSE:

People called "steady" are often only dense.

DENTISTRY:

The only thing worse
Than the dentist's drill
Is the size
When you get it
Of his bill.

Dentistry

DEPENDENCE AND INDEPENDENCE:

Dependence and independence are interdependent: The higher on the evolutionary scale the animal and, hence, the greater the potential for independence, the longer the period of infantile dependence.

DEPLANING:

The airplace has succeeded in obliterating the reason for its own existence. Now that we can go anywhere, anywhere has become like everywhere, and there is no reason to go.

DEPRESSION:

Very popular with the "in" crowd, having replaced nerves (in the '30's and '40's) and anxiety (in the '50's and '60's) as the disease of choice. Today, people who are not depressed are not worth knowing. Unfortunately, neither are people who are depressed.

DESCARTES:

Had Des cart before Des horse: I am, therefore I think, is the way it should have read.

DESIRE:

1. Almost no one knows what they want but they're all sure they haven't got it.

2. The only incurable disease.

3. Desire creates the world; thought annihilates it.

DESK-TOP PUBLISHING:

Has resulted in a hitherto unseen proliferation of paper in what was supposed to be a paperless society. We are swimming in newsletters up to our nuts if not our nipples. D.T.P. makes more, quicker, easier, and glitzier paper production possible, so more time can be spent on layout and design and less on content. No wonder we are drowning in dreck.

DETACHMENT:

The increasingly rare capacity not to be envious even if others have what we should be ashamed to own.

DETECTIVE STORIES:

1. These are often so alike that readers frequently find themselves inadvertently re-reading them: That which is quickly forgotten is readily repeatable.

2. If you wish to enjoy the finer points of a detective novel you should read the last chapter first. That way you can concentrate on the clues without worrying about "who dunnit."

DEVIANCE:

Individual deviance is tolerated where mass deviance is not. In a society where contradiction is the rule not the exception, this contradiction, too, is tolerated.

DEVELOPMENT:

The best synonym for "development" is "exploitation." Looking at most of the results of development, one is tempted to call it devilment.

DIAL-A-PRAYER:

1. Speed plead.

2. When convenience becomes a god, god becomes a convenience.

DIALECTICS OF ADVERTISING:

Advertising sells conformity as choice. The basic message is: Join us and become unique.

DIARRHEA:

Dire doings in the reah.

DIARY:

Mental diarrhea.

DICTATORIAL ATTITUDE:

What A denounces in B and practices on C.

DICTATORSHIP:

One man, one vote.

DIED OF BOREDOM:

Never given as the cause of death, although it may be the biggest killer of all.

DIETS:

1. Our principal form of self-indulgence.
2. The trouble with dieting is that people on a diet make less use of their mouth to eat and more use of their mouth to talk - usually about their diet.

DIFFERENCE:

Undress the rich and the poor and they are the same. It is poverty and riches which make us different, not difference which makes us rich or poor.

DIFFIDENCE:

Diffidence is not difficult; it's impossible.

DILDO:

A wife preserver.

DIOGENES:

Not a specially friendly guy - the lantern he carried gave light, not warmth.

DIRTY OLD MEN:

Is there another kind?

DISABILITY:

When you exclude the disabled, you don't necessarily exclude the weakest because weakness can be strength, just as strength can be weakness. The strongest leader America had in this century spent his days in a wheelchair.

DISAPPOINTMENT:

1. If you don't want to be disappointed, give up hope.

2. You'll never be disappointed if you always remember that whatever is, is wrong, and whatever happens, won't make it right.

DISASTER RELIEF:

Disasters bring out the best in people, thus, relieving those who had begun to believe that human nature is a disaster.

DISCONTENTED:

You are not truly discontented unless you envy someone enough to trade places with him. The unambitious envies the "other" while enjoying the indolence that places him beyond their reach.

DISCRETION:

When the boss tells you to "use your own discretion," she is really saying, "I don't want to be responsible."

DISCRIMINATION:

Poor old people always seem older than rich old people.

DISEASE:

The chief cure of boredom. When people become sick, they have something to think about: Things they have to do; things they can't do; things they should and shouldn't do. Getting sick is one of the best ways to get attention, care and poor.

DISEASE UNEASE:

Why is it that the disease you're treated for is rarely the disease that kills you?

DISHONESTY:

The honest thing would be to acknowledge our dishonesty. But that would deprive us of the pleasure of denouncing it in others. So, we prefer to *say* honesty is the best policy but to *practice* dishonesty. In this way, we get the best of both possible worlds: The real world, which is dishonest and the ideal world, which isn't.

DISOBEDIENCE:

You can only disobey what you acknowledge. What should be resented more than disobedience is disregard.

DISTRACTION:

1. We no longer solve problems, we switch stations.
2. The best therapy.

DISTURBANCE:

If you're not disturbed by others you have more time to disturb yourself.

DIVERSITY:

The latest fashion in conformity.

DIVINE WINE:

People who can't drink pity people who do drink. But it is incapacity not capacity that is to be pitied.

DIVORCE:

1. The prevalence of divorce may lead to a dangerous increase in happiness. The only remedy is remarriage.
2. Parents considering divorce should be placed in the custody of their children. They'd teach them how to behave.

DIVORCE AND REMARRIAGE:

Serial monotony.

DO-IT-YOURSELF:

Did we abolish the institution of slavery only to inflict it on ourselves?

DO-IT-YOURSELFER:

A person who prefers spending time to spending money; i.e., a cheapskate.

DOCTORATE:

It takes ten years to earn a doctorate which will get you a job (if you're lucky) paying about as much as a high school graduate earns.

DOERS:

People who can't relax - and can't stand people who can.

DOGMA:

1. Dogs flatter, lick, and obey (usually), feeding our egos. They kiss but never tell. And all they ask as a bonus is a bone.
2. There are dogs that growl at everything outside their cage and people who growl at everything above their stage.

DOGS:

Dogs may be servile, but people are imitative - which is only another kind of servility.

43

DOLE, ROBERT:

Known to his Best Enemies (he has few friends) as Robert Dull, he looks more doleful the older he gets. . .was probably on a government payroll (dole?) too long.

DOLLY PARTON:

The titular queen of country music.

DOMINATION (Capitalist Version):

When the law of rule is disguised as the rule of law.

DOO-DOO:

You have to take responsibility for your actions, they say. But "they" never take responsibility for their inaction. As many die from what we didn't do for them, but could have, as die from what we did do to them, but shouldn't have.

DOUBLE STANDARD:

Replaced the Gold Standard whose rigidity is said by some to have caused The Great Depression. Ever since we went on The Double Standard, we have avoided another Great Depression, even if we have not avoided war and a few other problems. So, let us thank God for The Double Standard which allows us to condemn in others what we condone in ourselves; Waste, deficits, lies, hyprocrisy, and all the other dead horses we enjoy flogging. Thank God, too, that we are too stupid to notice the contradiction.

DOUBT:

1. To think is to doubt; to believe is to dumb out.
2. Never doubt that all is in doubt.
3. The serious doubter finds in doubt new matter for doubt.

DOUBTFUL TRUTH:

The only truth there is - the search for truth begins with doubt, ends with doubt and is doubt.

DOWNSIZING:

1. Making people redundant. When do we start to upsize?
2. When corporations fire their employees, their stock soars; when governments report increased employment, stocks dive. Why don't we just fire everyone? That way, we'd all be rich.

DOWNTOWN:

Deadtown.

DREAMING:

What if we are someone else's dream?

DREAMING THE IMPOSSIBLE DREAM:

Women should *look* thin, but feel fat.

DREAMS:

Much can be learned from dreams. Unfortunately, no two people agree on what it is.

DRESS FOR SUCCESS:

With some people, undressing works better.

DRINKING:

I drink because I enjoy the good conversation it conduces to. Drinking is fine; it's driving that's the problem. To stay blissed out, stay blitzed-out.

Drinking

DRIVE-IN CHURCH:

Spreading the gaspol.

DROP-OUT:

The best lesson we learn in school is how little we learn in school. *That* lesson we learn when we are out of school. Your education begins when you drop-out.

DRUG-FREE AMERICA:

Are we sure we want this? It would not be a painless society.

DYSFUNCTIONAL FAMILY:

Freud got one thing right: Children need to rebel. For that to occur, nothing is more functional than a dysfunctional family.

E

EARLY:

Early to bed and early to rise won't necessarily make you healthy, wealthy, or wise. But you'll probably watch less television.

EARLY DEPARTURE:

If you wish to be remembered as a martyr, it helps to die young. If you do, people generally regard it as a tragedy; whereas, if you live too long, you may become a real pain in the ass, ridiculed and your death will be regarded with relief rather than regret. There *are* advantages to an early departure.

EARLY RETIREMENT:

1. When people can't wait to retire from a job, it means they didn't have a job, the job had them.
2. If you are considering early retirement you ought to re-read *King Lear.*

ECONOMIC DEVELOPMENT:

1. The rationalization is jobs, jobs, jobs; The aim is profits, profits, profits; The victim is environment, environment, environment.
2. From scenery to obscenery.
3. The gangrene spreads.

ECONOMIC PROJECTIONS:

When science becomes seance.

ECO-NOMICS:

When I see the way landfills are filling up, I figure we need to have more people unemployed, not less.

ECONOMISM:

When the social struggle is replaced by the job hunt; the search for a better world by the haggling over the 25 cent raise; the wider vision by narrow advantage; the movement by the vested interest; the community activist by the lobbyist lawyer; the volunteer by the careerist; the enthusiast by the bureaucrat; the commitment by the cash; socialism by self-seeking; leadership by office-holding; the true, the good and the beautiful by the quick, the convenient and the seductive; when sex is replaced by sexy; "accept no substitute" by virtual reality; heroes and heroines by stars and starlets; critical acclaim by starfucking; enlightenment by entertainment. Economism is the brave new world at the close of the 20th Century: A world in which intellectual, cultural and social values have regressed, been lowered and narrowed. The Old Left that refuses to acknowledge that it is as much affected by the decline as the Capitalism it deplores is not just hopeless, but retrograde. Its stupidity helps to keep us from seeing any light at the end of the tunnel.

ECUMENICISM:

Ten Gods offering tin goods.

EDUCATION:

Education

1. The process of forgetting everything you learned in school.
2. People believe in education. It's just that they prefer ignorance.
3. The educator should herself be educated.
4. Clinton thinks you can solve the problems of education by bringing back uniforms. It's called uniformity.

EFFICIENCY:

If you want your enterprise to look efficient, don't count all the costs.

THE EFFICIENT SOCIETY:

Since you're in it, I suppose that makes you inefficient.

EGYPTIAN DOCTOR:

Cairopractor.

EIGHT HUNDRED POUND GORILLAS:

Suffer from a bad press; they're peaceable vegetarians, after all.

THE EIGHTIES:

When the cost of selfishness went down and the cost of selflessness went up.

EJACULATIONS:

Fantasies in foam.

ELECTIBILITY:

You have to be able to walk the walk, talk the talk, and kiss the ass.

ELECTION:

Your chance to support someone you don't know, who promises what he cannot perform, and whose campaign is financed by the very vested interests busy bilking you.

ELECTION COVERAGE:

The idea is to cover politics as though it were a sport.

ELECTION RESULTS:

I used to find election results depressing until I noticed that they were meaningless.

ELECTIONS:

1. People want power. What they get instead is the vote.
2. There are no politics in America, only elections.

ELEGANCE:

When the choice is between elegance or intelligence, people chose the former, which proves they lack the latter.

ELEMENTARY TRUTH:

There is an element of truth in every doctrine.

ELITISM:

There is a difference between being an elitist and being a member of the elite. If you have taste, you're considered to be an elitist; if you have money, you're considered to be a member of the elite.

ELVIS:

Elvis Presley's resurrection has been announced more times than Jesus's. It is, in fact, possible that Elvis was (is?) Jesus. Still, the biggest miracle of all is that Jesus got as far as he did without a press agent.

EMBARRASSMENT:

It is really embarrassing when people take you too seriously. It's bad enough to be overlooked; it's far worse to be looked up to.

EMBOURGOISEMENT:

The adoption of the values of persons who have everything by persons who have nothing.

EMERGENCY MEDICINE:

This only came into its own with the rise in fatalities caused by modern weaponry, industry, and transport. Don't tell me that good doesn't come from bad!

EMERGENCY ROOM:

In civilized countries if you're bleeding, they treat you first and ask questions later. In America, if you're bleeding, they ask questions first and (depending on your insurance coverage) may or may not treat you - much later. Not to worry. Even if treated, you'll have a relapse when you get the bill.

EMPLOYEE RECOGNITION:

Recognition and praise - Cheaper than a raise.

EMPOWERMENT:

The latest fashion in enslavement.

ENDING DISCRIMINATION:

Discrimination doesn't happen if there are no statistics to document it; since we can't seem to stop discrimination, let's stop collecting statistics about it.

ENEMIES:

No two people need each other as much as enemies.

ENERGY-SAVING:

It takes less energy to despise circumstances than to hate them.

ENOUGH:

1. It used to be said, "enough is enough." Now, it is said, "You can't have enough." Apparently, we are only satisfied to be dissatisfied.
2. As much as you can get away with.

ENTERTAINMENT:

There's nothing entertaining about the entertainment business.

ENTHUSIASM:

You are considered "depressed" if you don't surrender to it; you will become depressed if you do.

ENVIRONMENTAL SOLICITATION:

50% green; 50% greed.

ENVIRONMENTAL IMPACT STATEMENT:

The real value of the E.I.S. is that it may tie up would-be polluters long enough to discourage them altogether. This is why the E.I.S. is better called the Environmental Impasse Statement.

ENVIRONMENTALISTS:

Every corporation now calls itself environmentalist. The defining question is: Does it act on the premise that the environment is a community or a commodity?

ENVY:

1. Envy arises from believing other people's bullshit about themselves.
2. If you wish you were someone else, you are really wishing you were dead.

EQUALITY I:

The President and the stockclerk of Wal-Mart's are equally entitled to Social Security benefits when they retire.

EQUALITY II:

A subtle change has occurred - the ideal of equality has been subverted. In its name everything is put on the same level: The paintings in the Sistine Chapel are no better than the graffiti on subway cars. What equality has come to mean is lowering the level; what it once meant was raising the level. A dog will piss on the tallest tree. Does that put him on its level?

EQUALITY OF OPPORTUNITY:

1. Anyone can be poor.
2. In this world, everyone is born equal to everyone else, but outgrows this very soon.

ETERNAL LIFE:

Now available - if you don't mind being tied to a tube. Soon they'll miniaturize and portabilize it, and you'll be able to buy it at Wal-Mart and earn Frequent Flyer miles.

EUROPE:

In Europe, the paper money has pictures of writers, thinkers, artists, and philosophers. In America, the paper money has pictures of politicians.

EVERYONE'S COMPLAINT:

Something's missing.

EVIL:

Whatever we dislike.

EVOLUTION:

1. The difference between animals and people is that animals are dumb but don't know it, and people are dumb but don't think it.
2. Darwin thought man descended from animals; Minsky thinks computers ascended from man.
3. Animals kill out of need. People just need to kill. Animals fight, but don't wage war. Only man, unique among the primates, practices large-scale, deliberate, enthusiastic, and systematic destruction of his fellow creatures. It isn't man's animal nature which is responsible for genocide, it is his society.

EVOLUTION AND REVOLUTION:

Animals don't have revolutions, only people do. Therein lies our hope.

EVOLUTIONARY APEX:

Man, the megalomaniacal monkey.

EXCEPTION:

There is an exception to every rule: Me.

EXCITEMENT:

If you can't get excited, at least get laid.

EXECUTIVE SECRETARY:

Corporate concubine.

EXERCISE:

The strange idea that you are "in control of your life" just because you have become *addicted* to mortifying the flesh. The trouble with exercise is that although it is good for reducing, it is also good for gaining. I never eat more than after exercising.

Exercise

EXIT:

Sartre's play, *No Exit* got it wrong. Life *is* a theatre, but there *are* exits. They just happen to be blocked right now.

EXOTIC FOOD:

Off the bitten track.

EXPECTATIONS:

Expectations are everything: Give a reader a newspaper and he complains if he doesn't get the gist of the story in the first sentence. Give the same reader a mystery story and he is satisfied if he's able to find out what it's really all about after 300 pages.

EXPERT:

1. A person who makes simple things complicated, thereby making himself indispensable.
2. Someone who's often done a thing inexpertly.

EXPERTS:

We are dependent on experts we don't trust, for opinions we don't like, about things we don't need. When there were fewer experts, there were fewer problems.

EXPLANATION:

I don't mean to complain, but I want to make it quite plain that to explain the obvious to the oblivious is a pain. Hence the expression, "painfully clear."

EXTENUATING CIRCUMSTANCE:

If you live in a cesspool, it's impossible to keep clean.

EXTERMINATOR'S SIGN:

In this house, we de-louse.

EXTERNALITIES:

The problems of development are viewed by economists as "externalities;" the problems of underdevelopment are viewed by them as immanent, which demonstrates the "con" in economics.

EYE CONTACT:

Doesn't always establish contact with the I.

F

FACING FACTS:

1. Just because you have to face facts, doesn't mean you have to like them. Anyway, it's not a matter of facing facts, but of managing them.
2. Facts are all very well as long as you mistrust them.

FACTIONALISM:

The clique shall inherit the earth.

FACTORY JOB:

Another day, another duller.

FACTS AND FIGURES:

The only things to believe in less than facts are figures.

FACTS OF LIFE:

No dough; No Perot.

FAILURE OF COMMUNICATION:

An all-purpose explanation. If people ask why anything failed, it can always be put down to Failure of Communication. The reason this explanation is accepted is because it is never *completely* untrue, however trivial a factor communication may have been. Besides, saying that something got screwed-up because of a failure of communication is less offensive than saying it was a stupid idea in the first place since a process is being blamed, not a person.

FAIR:

There are winners and there are losers, but what makes life fundamentally fair is that everyone loses in the end.

FAIR EXCHANGE:

1. If you can't solve a problem, exchange it.
2. Who needs faith when he can have doubt?

THE FAIR SEX:

What women used to be called until they started asking for fair treatment.

Fair Sex

FAITH:

1. To be a skeptic you need to have faith - in yourself.
2. Who wouldn't rather believe than face the fact that, in our time, Truth is a lie?
3. Wesley's spiritual teacher, Boehler told him: "Preach faith until you have it; then you will preach it because you have it." In a word, suggestion is the basis of faith.

FAITH OF A CYNIC:

He would have believed anything bad said about anybody, except that he knew everybody was a liar. His faith in people was based on cynicism.

FAITHFULNESS:

In dogs it's wonderful, but if ladies want faithfulness in men, they'll have to neuter them. . .which would seem to defeat the purpose.

FALSIFIABILITY:

Science can be refuted; religion can't - which is why science is preferable, the criterion of the true being the false.

FAME:

1. Andy Warhol's most famous remark was that we would all have our 15 minutes of fame. Infamy is more like it. The limelight has become the slimelight. You no longer have to be in high places to be accused of high crimes: The colossal maw of the media requires an unending supply of victims.
2. When your name becomes well-known, it's time to change it.
3. Fame, today, is more often bought than earned. The exceptions are mostly accidents based on misunderstandings.

FAMILY BUSINESS:

Since the heirs are invariably epigones, the family business rarely survives the demise of its founder.

FAMILY VALUE OR THE VALUE OF FAMILIES:

It's best to borrow money from those who may have difficulty asking for it back. . .hey, what's a family for, anyway?

FAMILY VALUES:

Christians who preach Family Values tend to forget that Jesus told His disciples to abandon *their* families and follow Him.

FAMINE:

Famine in the Third World makes it much easier to dismiss poverty in the first world.

FAMOUS:

There are nine things you can be sure of if you become famous:
1. Blackmail;
2. Gossip;
3. Death threats;

4. Marriage proposals;
5. Envy;
6. The emergence of relatives you never knew you had;
7. Requests for money;
8. Calls from brokers;
9. Ultimate neglect.

FANATICISM:

Irrefutable.

FASHION:

It's no longer fashionable to be old.

FAST FACTS ABOUT FAST FOOD RESTAURANTS:

Low salaries; high calories.

FAT:

1. The problem with being fat is that people don't take you seriously.
2. Time enough to be a skeleton when you're dead.

FAT-FREE:

1. What we need even more than a fat-free diet is a fad-free diet.
2. Fast-food restaurants are really fat-food restaurants.
3. To avoid fat, eat lots of beans: More fart, less fat.
4. If everything is now fat-free, why are the number of fat-heads increasing?

FAT PEOPLE:

Fat people are the lepers of a society run by fatheads.

FATALISM:

When the fatalist philosopher beat the slave for stealing his bread, the slave protested, "Your own philosophy proves that I was fated to lift it. Why do you beat me?" To which the philosopher replied, "If you were fated to steal my bread, I was fated to beat your head."

FATE:

When something goes wrong we blame it on fate. When something goes right *we* take the credit.

FATHER ARISTIDE:

Clinton seems to have a love and haiti relationship with him.

FEAR:

It is the fear of being alone that drives the herd; it is the fear of not being alone that drives the individual.

FEAR AND LOVE:

When you fear someone, you try to figure them out; when you love someone, you don't even want to try - you're too busy enjoying them. Fear is a greater spur to truth than love.

FEDERAL DEFICIT:

Borrowing for the political payoffs of today from the non-existent revenues of tomorrow.

FEDERAL DEFICIT OR THINKING DEFICIT:

1. If the government didn't buy stuff from the private sector, there'd be no deficit.
2. The Crash of '29 took place when the budget was in surplus which suggests that Keynes was right after all: The reason we haven't had a recurrence of the Big One is that we've been in deficit ever since.
3. Businesses go out of countries, countries don't go out of business.

FATHER DIVINE:

A minister to the poor; not a poor minister.

FEEDBACK:

An echo chamber.

FEEL GOOD:

If you want to feel good, cop a good feel.

FEMINIST FLUMMERY:

If you can say "my mother," why can't you say "my wife?"

FENCE:

A receiver of stolen goods. A philanthropist is a donor of same.

FESTSCHRIFT:

Ideas in a tome designed to serve as their tomb.

FETISH:

You can make a fetish out of anything: Love, Truth, Beauty, Goodness, Feet...

FETUS:

A fully formed human being said by anti-abortionists to possess a soul, personality, intelligence, a sense of humor and very definite ideas about the difference between right and wrong. Should be given the right to vote, a credit card, a driver's license, and a job.

FICTION:

1. You can "get away" with more and bigger truths in fiction than in non-fiction. Why? If you write fiction, you won't be sued.
2. Fiction is to fact what dreaming is to thinking. Both are natural and necessary.
3. Fiction gives existence to the non-existent, thereby ceasing to be fiction and becoming fact.

FIDELITY:

A virtue exclusive to Fido.

FIELDS, W.C.:

The Wizard of Booze.

FIGURE-SKATING:

1. In the wake of the Harding-Kerrigan affair some have wondered if figure skating is not really girls' ice-hockey.
2. A mixture of muscle, movement, and music to produce multi-million dollar commercial endorsements, as the icing on the take, so to speak.
3. Iced heist.

FILM:

What creeps over your eyes as you watch most movies.

FIRST PRINCIPLE OF SELECTION:

Select very carefully what you can discard very easily.

FIRST PRINCIPLES:

There are no first principles. There are principles *we* place first.

FIRSTISM:

The thirst to be first is an exercise in futility. Whenever it is proven that "X" did "it" first, someone comes along to claim that "Y" preceded him. People can't get used to thinking of life as a circle in which the first is last.

FLATTERY:

1. If you fuck up, suck-up. Flattery will get you everywhere and is dangerous only if *you* believe it.
2. Flatter with gifts, not words. That way you can't be accused of lying.

FLEALESS DOGS:

Long conversations that do not include at least a few lies are about as likely as dogs without fleas.

FLIGHT TO FLORIDA:

The flight from the North to Florida is a flight from variety to monotony; from four seasons to one; from hill and dale to flat and flatter, from hot to steamy. But, of course, it's relatively cheap. Florida's popularity is an example of how the money culture makes people gravitate to monoculture.

FLORIDA:

Ponce de Leon discovered the Fountain of Youth in Florida. Seeking the fabled Fountain, the elderly are drawn to the penis-shaped state like flies to shit. Drying in the endless, unforgiving sun, they turn into copper coins that have been tossed, then lost in the Fountain.

FLOSSING:

Not just a matter of plaque and white.

FLUORIDATION:

Was supposed to poison us. Unfortunately, it didn't work.

FOLLOWER:

If followers don't sometimes lead, leaders fall and followers follow. But while fallen leaders tend to get picked up, fallen followers tend to stay down.

FOREIGN AID:

Welfare for the corporate sector. The major beneficiaries of foreign aid are not the foreigners. Here's how it works: We advance the foreign country credit which it can use to buy what we export. In that way, we buy the country in exchange for their buying our goods - with our money. That is to say, the American taxpayer (which rarely means American corporations - since their tax burden gets lower each year, while the tax burden of the middle-class increases) buys American goods for the foreign country. Unfortunately, those goods or goodies are rarely appropriate to those countries; indeed, they cause a multitude of problems - social, environmental, political, ethical, and financial - which often lead to civil wars and military adventures we may be invited to help solve (since we helped cause them). If there are winners in this process, they are, in order of importance:

1. American corporations, whose sales abroad are underwritten by American taxpayers;
2. Politicians, who pass the enabling legislation and get donations from the corporations that benefit;
3. A few officials of foreign governments, who benefit politically and financially over and/or under the table. I would not call this foreign aid. And while you may call it charity, I prefer the word subsidy. Or, domestic assistance. Or, welfare.

FOREIGN POLICY:

Don't wrong the strong; Tweak the weak.

FOREPLAY:

More fun when four play.

FOREST MANAGEMENT:

It's not the forests that need to be managed, but the loggers.

FOREST RANGER:

Thinking is dreaming along paved paths; dreaming is thinking along footpaths.

FORGETFULNESS:

Of all the weights that crush us, the weight of the past is heaviest. So, while forgetfulness is commonly considered a defect, I consider it a gift from God. What else lightens the load of past error, sin, and folly?

FORMULA FICTION:

1. *Detective Story:* Victims: Many; Villians: Plenny; Drinks: Genny; Fucks: Any.
2. *Romance:* Skintillating saga of scantily arrayed maid and scantily-clad lad.
3. *Western:* Dialogue: Flat; Plot: Rot; Characters: Threadbare except for the mare.

FORMULA PHRASE:

"I don't want to sound cynical." Really? Then, why are you trying so hard to be clever?

FOUNDATIONS (Philanthropic):

Just because you know how to accumulate money doesn't mean you know what to do with it. Energy in getting greatly exceeds wisdom in giving.

FOX:

Should never be put in the chicken soup.

FRANCE:

France can be forgiven many things for its wines, cheeses, sauces, perfumes, style, and accent.

FREE:

We never feel more free than after we have paid our taxes, been released from jail or concluded the work week. Is slavery a precondition for freedom?

FREE AT LAST:

Did Martin Luther King, Jr. mean fat-free, sugar-free, salt-free, or cholesterol-free? Because, politically, socially, or economically free, we're not.

FREE CHOICE:

If it's free, it's rarely choice.

FREE PRESS:

I'm not sure whether what we have is a free press or a press that's free with the truth.

FREE SCREECH:

The worst place to work is one where the radio blares all day. Between the Schlock and Roll, the shrill advertisements, and the noise called News, you can lose it. Is it just my imagination or do people speak louder now, because they have gotten into the habit of talking over radios and TV's? If you complain about any of this, free speech is invoked. Shouldn't it be called Free Screech?

FREE SPEECH:

Means being able to say anything to anyone at anytime - except "fire" in a crowded theatre. "Fire" is the only four-letter word that is forbidden.

FREE TELEVISION:

Free of taste, intelligence, and wit.

FREE TRADE:

Said to be the solution to all our problems - except that there is no such thing. It's a myth, like the myth of "the free lunch." But while the latter is ridiculed ("There's no such thing as a free lunch"), the former is deified. It's interesting to conjecture why that is...perhaps because our masters have an interest in promoting the myth of free trade but none in promoting the myth of the free lunch since the former makes them money, while the latter costs them money. Every significant industry and business is directly and/or indirectly subsidized. In a word, free trade is a principle and you know how it is with principles: They are goals we strive (not) to reach, but to preach.

FREE WILL:

We're tossed about like leaves in a storm. But if leaves could speak, they'd probably boast about their free will.

FREEDOM:

1. The right to enslave others.
2. What is needed is more freedom from profit and less freedom to profit.

FREEDOM FIGHTER:

Spends the first part of his life fighting for freedom and the last part of his life wondering where, what, and if it is.

FREEDOM OF CHOICE:

The patient's sacred right to choose his own doctor about whose credentials, experience, education, malpractice problems, or skills he knows next to nothing. Sometimes referred to as "informed choice."

FREEDOM OF EXPRESSION:

1. The right to be wrong.
2. We're all for freedom of expression until we meet someone who can't govern her tongue.
3. Freedom of expression does not include telling children to cross the street against the light.

FREEDOM OF INFORMATION:

1. Before The Information Explosion, I believed devoutly in Freedom of Information. Now, I believe in Freedom from Information.
2. The freedom of the media to make up stories.

FREEDOM OF REPRESSION:

The very latest freedom. It means that any organized group can say anything about itself, including racial slurs, ethnic jokes and gender put-downs, but people outside this group can only say nice things about it. Once called the double standard, this is now referred to as Freedom of Repression.

FREUD:

A scientist he wasn't; his theories are unprovable and worse, unfalsifiable. So, who was Freud? A great religious leader. He founded a religion for the enlightened bourgeosie in an age when the educated found it hard to swallow traditional religion any longer. The old myths might be O.K. for the peasants, but the intelligentsia had to have them flavored with scientific sounding neologisms like "forces," "drives," "instincts," "Id," "superego," etc. If these were not mystical, they were at any rate mystifying.

FREUD SIMPLIFIED:

Get a good lay and you'll feel O.K.

FRIENDSHIP:

1. If you have one true friend in your life, you're lucky; two is a miracle; three a mirage.
2. It isn't as though friendship has no price: An oft-bitten tongue.

FRUITOPIA:

Where apple-cheeked vegetarians go when they die.

FRUSTRATION:

Arises out of the discrepancy between knowledge and power.

FUNDAMENTALISM:

What the ascendence of Fundamentalism signals is that God has completed a strategic withdrawal from the world, leaving it entirely in the hands of advanced nut-cases, who raise money and hell in His name. Having given up hope of making this world better, He has apparently retreated to the next world. Who can blame Him? It was either that or take a chance on being nailed to the cross again by the storm-troopers of the religious right.

FUNDAMENTALIST:

A pain in the fundament.

THE FUNDAMENTALS:

Invoked in every speech, ignored in every action. Appearances are much more important than fundamentals and nothing makes a better appearance than talking about fundamentals.

FUNDRAISERS:

Used to be called beggars.

FUNDRAISER'S FAITH:

Buried deep inside every rich person are seeds of self-doubt plus a puzzled wonderment at a world which lets him get away with his ill-gotten gains. It is these tender shoots that the fundraiser carefully cultivates and wishfully waters.

FUNDRAISING:

It is begun to secure money for charitable endeavors, but eventually it turns into its opposite: Charitable endeavors come to exist for the purpose of raising funds.

FUNERAL:

To think that I had lunch with him only yesterday!? How old was he, exactly? So young? [said, no matter how old he was.] He had so much to live for. Why him? [You'd have preferred maybe his brother?] Were there many people at the funeral? How many? *That* many! Did his ex-wife come? Were there a lot of flowers? It was all for the best [in the best of all possible worlds, doubtless]. What a shame. He had a full life. Just when he had begun to live [I thought you just said he had a *full* life]. Doesn't he look good? [Well, for a corpse, he does.] At least he won't suffer any more [unless he can hear this conversation].

FUNERALS:

1. There's nothing quite like someone else's funeral for making one's own life look better.
2. Better she than me.

FUNEREAL:

The face we wear at the funeral of the friend we wanted nothing to do with for the past 20 years:
> *Shoulders sagging*
> *Bellies bagging*
> *Noses blowing*
> *Into ragging.*
> - I. Snivel.

Thus, do we carry ourselves gravely to the grave, overcome by the gravity of the situation, and, indeed by the entire Farce Of Gravity.

THE FUTURE:

1. You shouldn't spend any time worrying about it. You're much better off undermining it.
2. I have seen the future and it sucks.
3. There *is* night at the end of the tunnel.

FUTURE SCHLOCK:

1. When men and women will be replaced by money and machines. We're almost there.
2. What socialism was at the beginning of the 20th Century, environmentalism is at its close; the latter having replaced the former in the affection of the disaffected. Environmentalism may suffer the same fate as socialism - that of having a marginal, largely rhetorical effect on events. Meanwhile, pollution grows and spreads like crazy, (withal unevenly) as it must under capitalism, triumphing everywhere...its triumphs are hollow, of course, and its social costs enormous - far exceeding its benefits. But who's counting anything except the profits that inure to the few? Anyway, when did waste, carnage, vulgarity, brutality, and futility ever discourage energy and enterprise? The show must go on - even if and especially if it is mostly show...This is not to say environmentalism is wrong any more than socialism was wrong. But whether an idea is right or wrong has little to do with its actual influence.

FUTURE SHOCK:

If you really want to know what your future will be like, visit the cemetery.

FUTUROLOGY:

1. Science fiction minus the science.
2. Futurologists are very proud of their correct predictions...as well they should be, considering how few they make.
3. The future is forever hidden from us. The futurologist is the striptease artist, who raises a corner of the veil. The enduring allure of prophecy is its teasing quality not its revelatory power.

G

G-SPOT:

If you think spotting the Spotted Owl is hard, try spotting the G-Spot.

GADFLY:

A fly that bites cattle. Since the herd keeps growing, more gadflies are needed.

GAMBLING:

1. Having children in today's world.
2. The last, best hope of the desperate: If you have neither money, brains or talent, where else would you worship except at the shrine of Our Lady of Luck?
3. We are witness to a tremendous explosion of gambling in our time: Gambling increases as misery, boredom, stupidity, and superstition increase.

GAME:

Everything is now called a game because games have become like everything: Business. "Fun and games" - the two used to go together. No more. The fun has gone out of games since they have become super-organized, smothered in layers of bureaucracy, replete with rules, Commissioners, public relations experts, legal and financial counsel, medical and psychological specialists, marketing mavens, deal-makers, agents, TV contracts, multi-million dollar commercial endorsements, big-time betting, etc. We're not talking game, we're talking gain.

GARDENING:

If you're paid to do it, it's work; if you pay to do it, it's play.

GARLIC:

The new HOT HEALTH food: it's not what's in the garlic that makes it healthy. It's the smell: If you eat enough of it no one will come near, so you can't catch their germs.

GENDER GIP:

The reason women work harder is that men are the weaker sex.

GENEALOGICAL RESEARCH:

The tribute we pay to our forebears in the hope, usually vain, that those who follow, will pay us tribute.

GENEROUS:

A word that is applied too generously.

GENIAL:

Genuinely genial people are those who give us both a sense of what life is like and of what it should be like - they teach us how to live without hope at the same time as they fill us with hope.

GENTLEMAN:

It is often said that there are no gentlemen left. But if we should, by some miracle find one, we are quick to apologize and tell people that "really, he is tough." A *tough* gentleman? Hmmm.

Gentleman

GENIUS:

So, what's *wrong* with him?

GEORGE WILL:

He won't.

GEOGRAPHY AND HISTORY:

Late 19th Century America had the Wild West; Late 20th Century Russia is the Wild East.

GESTALT:

The notion that the whole is more than the sum of its parts; e.g., 1 + 1 equals 3.

GETTING AWAY WITH SOMETHING:

What really bothers me when somebody gets away with something is that it isn't me.

GIFT:

I've never received a gift that I haven't paid for in one way or another.

GINGRICH:

A newt that is not mute.

GIVE 'EM WHAT THEY WANT:

Giving people what they want is certain to kill off individuality, since in mass society what everybody wants is what the next guy has no matter how stupid it is. Let's call things by their proper names - giving people what they want is not democracy, it is pandering. If you want what you know something about, you know what you want. If you don't know anything about it beyond what the advertisers have told you, you don't know shit - which is what you get.

GLOOM AND DOOM:

Probably the title of an Ingmar Bergman movie.

GNU:

Q. Nu, so what's gnu?
A. Nothing, But no gnu's is good gnus.

GO GO GUY:

If you wake up in the morning raring to go - go back to sleep.

GOALS:

Not to be enslaved by goals is the only truly satisfying goal.

GOALS AND OBJECTIVES:

Sometimes abbreviated G.O.O. - and for goo reason.

GOD:

1. God knows.
2. Non-entity as supreme entity.
3. Of course, God isn't real. Why would She want to be? Anybody can be real.

GOD IS DEAD:

That's why Goddess religion is flourishing.

GOD IS LOVE:

You can say God is love, but you shouldn't say Love is God.

GOING INTO BUSINESS FOR ONESELF:

"I'll go into business so I can be my own boss." The Great Illusion of the fed-up ambitious. Once you have "your" own business you are enslaved by the banks, have to kiss the customers' asses, bribe the suppliers and stroke the employees. You end by exploiting members of your own family as well as yourself - all in the name of "being your own boss." Moral: There's no such thing as being your own boss. Every boss has a boss: Adam had Eve; Bill has Hillary.

GOING TO GRADUATE SCHOOL:

From neighborhood bar to seminar.

GOOD:

What people who have missed their opportunities like to think they are.

GOOD, BAD, AND BEAUTIFUL:

We can't all be beautiful, but we can all be good. What is bad is that more people try to be beautiful than good.

GOOD CAUSE:

Why is it that the only good cause you feel really good about is the one you helped cause?

GOOD DEED:

No good deed goes unpunished.

GOOD HABITS:

Those who exercise, eat the right foods, and abstain from liquor, vice and tobacco lead a long life: But the longest life is led by those already dead.

GOOD INTENTIONS:

We all have good intentions. The question is: Good for whom?

GOOD LIFE:

The good life is thought by many to be one in which all your thinking and work are done for you by good people.

GOOD NEWS:

Good is attainable; evil endurable. For that matter, evil is attainable and good is endurable.

GOOD NEWS/BAD NEWS JOKE:

The good news is that we're living longer. The bad news is that we're living longer.

GOODBYE TO THE HEREAFTER:

The masses don't believe in Heaven any longer. They have Wal-Mart now. The masses don't believe in Hell, either. There is downsizing instead.

GOODNESS:

It's harder to write a good sentence than to be good.

GORDIAN KNOT:

It's like I always said: Some people just can't cut it.

GOVERNMENT:

A seat for every ass; an ass for every seat.

GOVERNMENT WASTE:

Anything that helps the poor. If it helps the rich then it's not called waste, it's called investment.

GRADE SYSTEM:

Grading is a substitute for judging which is why it is so popular. Anything that enables us to avoid thinking is bound to be popular.

GRADUATE:

Is there any intelligence left beneath the layers of acquired ignorance?

GRADUATION:

"They" tell you you can't get a job if you don't graduate. But then "they" complain that graduates can't spell, write, read, talk, add, or subtract, don't know geography, history, science, or current events, and lack common sense and experience. So, how come they don't hire drop-outs?

GRAMMAR:

Allz you every see is people whom don't no there gramma.

GRANDEUR:

We seek grandeur in nature because it's so hard to find in people.

GRANTSMANSHIP:

1. Getting new money to continue old activities under a new name.
2. It's harder to get money to continue or improve something that's working than it is to get money for something new and unproved. Apparently, the unproved is considered improved.

GRATITUDE:

You don't have to feel grateful to the state for anything. You ought to feel grateful to the state for that.

GREAT FAITH:

Usually accompanied by little learning.

GREED:

1. Even greed has its good side: Greedy people don't commit suicide; they won't give *anything* up.
2. One of the few things left you can absolutely count on.
3. Generally speaking, greed now explains more about people's behavior than need. It used to be the other way 'round. That's progress.

GREENHOUSE EFFECT:

Especially noticeable those years we don't experience an Ice Age.

GREETING CARD:

Invented to cover the difficulty of feigning grief and joy...not everyone is an actor...

GRIDLOCK:

Used to be called the System of Checks and Balances.

GRIN AND BARE IT:

Dentists smile a lot not because they're happy, but because they're advertising.

GROUNDS FOR HOPE:

We live only a short time.

GROUP SEX:

What they did in the '60's before AIDS was invented. Has been replaced by grope sex.

GROWING OLD:

You know you're growing old when the wee hours become the wee wee hours.

GROWN-UP:

I used to think people were stupid. Now I know it.

GROWTH:

When you change, but the people you grew up with don't, they think you have betrayed them when, in fact, they have betrayed themselves.

GROWTH INDUSTRIES:

Who says America has no growth industries? What about Repressed Memory Syndrome, Attention Deficit Disorder, Obsessive Compulsive Disorder, Hyperactivity, or Irritable Bowel Syndrome?

GUIDELINE:

If you want to enjoy people, don't take them seriously.

GUILT:

Rarely lasts more than a week - unlike shame, which rarely lasts more than a day.

GUILTY VERDICT:

Usually pronounced by those who didn't get caught on those who did.

GULF WAR:

Some say it was fought to preserve a cheap, steady supply of oil for the West. I say it was fought to preserve the world for oil - Big Oil. It is entirely possible that The Gulf War was a made-for-television movie, starring Dick, er - Colin Powell.

GUNICIDE:

What you got when genocide crossed the ocean and came to the United States.

GURU:

1. A four-letter synonym for charlatan.
2. What should be said to a guru is, "Shaman you!"

H

HALF-TRUTHS:

All truths are half-truths; all half-truths are quarter truths; all quarter truths are lies.

HAIR:

It seems hard to believe today that the major causes of strife in the '60's were long hair on men and short skirts on women. There are other theories that purport to account for the turmoil of those times but the long and short of it is provided by this theory.

HAIRCUT:

It is terribly important to keep your hair properly trimmed. Sloppy hair is the sign of a sloppy mind. Einstein proved this definitively.

Haircut

HANDICAPPED PARKING:

Handicapped access is one thing; handicapped excess quite another.

HANDWRITING:

Best seen on a wall.

71

HAPPINESS:

1. "I'm only thinking about your happiness." The most common phrase appended to any proposal designed to create abject misery for the person to whom it is addressed.
2. Happiness is not a condition, it's an attitude. Bliss is not a state, it's a feeling. Paradise is not a place, it's a judgment.

> *Resting roundly on one's rear*
> *is a pastime very dear.*
> *To Pope, To peasant, To Emir,*
> *That at least, is very clear.*

HAPPY ENDINGS:

Endings are only happy in the movies. In real life, they're haphazard.

HAPPY FACE:

Pleasant, smiling people are best for committing high crimes and misdemeanors and getting away with them. Compare the treatment given rosy Reagan with that meted out to nasty Nixon - even though Iran-Contra maimed many more than Watergate.

HAPPY HOUR:

They had a drink or two and pleasantly pissed the day away.

HAPPY PEOPLE:

I have met many, many happy people in my life. Unhappily, they were all deluded.

Happy Hour

HAPPY THOUGHT:

Things have a tendency to organize themselves and organizations have a tendency to become disorganized.

HAPPYCHONDRIA:

I used to get sick a lot - until I discovered better ways to enjoy myself.

HARD LABOR:

Making little rocks out of big rocks.

HARLEY DAVIDSON'S HOG HEAVEN:

"Biking is the closest thing to freedom you can get," said the long-haired, beer-bellied Baron astride his big bike. He was clad in black helmet, black leather jacket, spiked black suede boots and had a black visor over his face. His similarly attired blond companion in black bikini top, nodded assent. They were members of The Christian Motorcycle Association (I couldn't make this up) whose motto, emblazoned on their metallic steed, was, "Riding For The Son," and they were in D.C. for the 7th Annual Rolling Thunder Parade. One thing about "biking" is that it's democratic. "Practically anyone can bike," a blackshirted Hunk, aged 84 told me. Bikers like to call themselves "hogs" and considering the noise, fumes, and hazards they create, they have indeed contributed their own not inconsiderable bit to turning the world into a pigsty. Still, Harley-Davidson is an American Success Story - the last motorcycle manufacturer left in the States. Like I always say, the only thing that will save us is a major depression.

HAT:

The industry that J.F.K. killed because he refused to wear one. He was probably killed by a bitter unemployed hatter. This is the only conspiracy theory that has *not* (up to now) been advanced to account for the assassination. It is also the most plausible one: An unemployed hatter would have had both motive and importunity.

HATE:

The tie that binds *because* it divides. What the Irish do best is hate the English.

HATE THY NEIGHBOR:

2,000 years of "love thy neighbor" has yielded us exactly what? Isn't it time to try a new approach? What people say is what they *don't* do. Therefore, I offer "Hate Thy Neighbor" as the watchword for the 21st Century. Variants might include: "Be Happy with your Hatred" and "Hate Thy Neighbor as Thyself." (Self-hatred replacing self-esteem, which I think is too esteemed.) Or, how about, "I never met anyone I couldn't hate." I suggest, too, a new political party: The Hate For Happiness Movement.

HATEFUL TRUTH:

Children who hate school are learning to live with hate.

HAWAII:

When you step off the plane in Honolulu, they stick a lei around your neck. It's called getting lei'd.

HEADLINES:

Happiness gets no headlines.

HEALING:

In the therapeutic culture, everyone seeks "healing." It's a sick thing to do, since there are more victims of the "healing process" than there are people healed by it.

HEALING THE HEELS:

If you are well-heeled, you are well-healed.

HEALTH:

1. Everyone wants it. No one has it. Rene Dubos was right 35 years ago when he called it a "mirage." The best health cure would be a cure for "health."
2. Trying too hard to be healthy will only make you sick.

HEALTH CARE:

1. The most profitable business of all - the demand never dries up. An even more profitable business than sex, which, if you live long enough, ultimately does dry up.
2. There is no evidence that people who get more health care are any healthier. The only thing one can say with certainty is that the more doctors and hospitals there are, the more money is spent on health care. The moral may be that though more practitioners may not be better for you, it is better for them.

HEALTH CARE SYSTEM IN AMERICA:

About as effective as a leaky condom.

HEALTH FOOD:

You know that it comes from the health food store if it looks cheap, costs dear, and is worm-eaten. Apparently the worms know that beauty is only skin deep, which is why they don't shop at the supermarket.

HEALTH INSURANCE:

In America, this means the insurance industry is healthy.

HEARTY LAUGHTER:

Starts in the stomach and ends on the floor.

Hearty Laughter

HEDONISM:

Heed the happy hedonist - a sinless society is a sunless society.

74

HEIRS AND EPIGONES:

Stalin was to Lenin what Paul was to Jesus.

HELL:

1. "Abandon all hope, you who enter," is supposed by Dante to be the inscription on the gate to Hell. But wouldn't that also have to be the inscription on the gate to Heaven? After all, if we still had to depend on hope, what would be the point of going to Heaven?
2. Say what you will about it, Hell is one place where you don't have to worry about keeping warm.

HELP-WANTED ADS:

Why is it that they list all the qualifications except the ones most needed: Confidence, courage, humor, cunning, and fortitude?

HEMORRHOIDS:

You can always tell who's suffering from hemorrhoids. It's the one who's "sitting pretty."

HENRY KISSINGER:

When they gave him the Prize for Peace, it took all the Nobelity out of it...but then Alfred made his dough in dynamite.

HENRY THE EIGHTH:

Would have served him right if *he'd* married Lorena Bobbitt.

HEREAFTER:

Clov: Do you believe in the life to come?
Hamm: Mine was always that.
Beckett: Endgame

HERESY:

1. What the musical *Hair* was to the Marine Corps.
2. The true heretic accepts nothing she cannot test. In a word, she has testes.

HEROES:

1. Heroes are necessary - in novels.
2. I don't want to be a hero - neither do I want to be a zero.
3. The only reason to consider being a hero is that dying a natural death may impair your prospects for advancement in the afterlife.

HIGH FIDELITY:

When veracity turns into voracity: Fidelity to what? High fidelity is sound that never existed in the real world; hyper-fidelity - hyped-up, souped-up sound. It is faithful to the point of being distorted - a prime example of how things at their extreme turn into their opposite. Now you know where the expression, "faithful to a fault" comes from.

HIGH-TECH:

Used to be the way to solve problems. Now it's the way to create them.

HIGH-TECH JOBS:

The Administration is very hot for this, but there may be less here than meets the eye. High-tech is the *replacement,* in many cases, of people by computers. "Jobs, Jobs, Jobs," doesn't necessarily mean full employment. For *that* to happen, you also need low-tech and no-tech jobs: The kind there never seems to be any money for, even though there's a social need. Moreover, these are the kinds of jobs compensated so poorly, people prefer welfare. The fixation on high-tech fixes, the obsession with "information super-highways," the gravitation to gimmickry, the illusion that improved technology will solve all social problems - what is this but the ages-old illusion of technocracy?

HIGHWAYS:

Thanks to the interstate highway system, it's possible to travel across the country without seeing anything. Thanks to the information superhighway, it's possible to travel across the spectrum of knowledge without understanding anything.

HI-HO FINANCE:

Junk bonds and Derivatives are just the tip of the sheisberg.

HILLARY RODHAM CLINTON:

The Cheshire Cat as First Lady.

HIPPOCRATIC HYPOCRISY:

Above all, do no harm. . .to the physician's income.

HIROSHIMA AND NAGASAKI:

To err is Truman.

HIRSUTE:

Tailored woman.

HISTORY LESSON:

The lesson of history is that there is no lesson of history.

HISTORY UP TO NOW:

So far, no good.

HITS:

There are hits in the Sicilian sense and hits in the Broadway sense.

HIV NEGATIVE:

Immaculate ejaculate.

HOLISTIC HEALTH:

The desire to make one's life a "coherent whole" is doomed to failure. "Coherent whole," my ass!...Indeed, that may be the only coherent hole there is...

THE HOLY TRINITY:

Quick, easy, and cheap.

THE HOLY TRINITY REVISITED:

Money, power, and sex.

HOME:

A man's home is his castle: Drafty, leaky, old, unlivable, and the taxes are too high. But there's moat to it than that.

THE HOMELESS:

1. (View by editorial page writer for *The Wall Street Journal*) "The worst thing we can do for the Homeless is to house them. They'd lose their identity. If we clothed or fed them, as knee-jerk liberals tearfully tell us to, our streets would no longer be filled with colorful, pungent people. For street life, you need street people. Besides, if people want to freeze to death or starve, let them. I, for one, refuse to be patronizing or to belittle their miserable way of life by providing for them. Generally speaking, people get what they deserve: They deserve shit; I deserve a raise."
2. In the Middle Ages, they were called, "Holy men" or hermits.
3. The derelict society is not as driven as the driven society, which may be one reason the driven society is derelict in its duty to the derelict.

HOMELESSNESS:

A whole host of callings that once provided a modest home plus a modest income for doing what was *intermittently* useful have been eliminated: Jobs such as lighthouse keeper, stationmaster, canal locksman. Moreover, the number of church livings have been reduced. Supposedly, we can no longer afford to provide affordable housing (except in prisons) for the poor, or even the working poor. But we can afford to provide free palaces for those who could easily afford to own their own: College presidents and heads of large eleemosynary institutions - for example.

HOMICIDE:

1. Urban renewal.
2. The bad news is that the rates keep climbing; the good news is that if they keep climbing at high-enough rates, the population problem may be solved.

HOMOSEXUALITY:

Considered by some to be "unnatural" although it occurs everywhere in nature and is found throughout history.

HONEST:

When a book is described as "thoroughly honest," you know it will be boring.

HONESTY:

1. Honesty is the best policy - except when policy is better than honesty.
2. When honesty becomes a matter of policy, it soon ceases to be honesty.

HONKY:

Melanin deprived.

HONORABLE MENTSCHEN:

Jack Kevorkian, Noam Chomsky, Thomas Szasz.

HOPE:

1. Sometimes spelled "hype."
2. A deliberate decision to deny all that you have ever learned from history and your own experience. If you have hope, you are definitely "in denial." I feel so much better now that I've given it up.
3. An inexpensive way of prolonging agony.
4. Hope is a source of most delusion and delusion is the source of most hope.
5. So long as people can still make mistakes, there is still hope.

6. If one wishes to avoid disappointment, a life without hope may be the best one can hope for.

HOSPITALS:

People used to die at home, now they die in hospitals. It must be because the DIEt is better there.

HOUSING:

Big cities stimulate without satisfying; little cities satisfy without stimulating; suburbs are better for cars than people; rural areas, once quiet, clean, and pretty, are becoming landfills. The only livable place is inside your own head. Make sure it's well furnished. Read a good book.

HUBRIS:

Washington can't solve the Civil War raging five blocks from the Capitol, but thinks it can solve Civil Wars 10,000 miles away.

HUMAN NATURE:

Whether man is by nature good or bad is largely a function of whether his society is good or bad. When a father enquired about the best method of educating his son in ethical conduct, a Pythagorean replied: "Make him a citizen of a state with good laws." Ours is a state with *many* laws.

HUMAN POTENTIAL MOVEMENT:

Helps us realize our full potential - usually for evil. Be all that you can be is the slogan. Take all that you can take is the reality.

HUMANITIES:

The function of the humanities in the contemporary university is ornamental.

HUMIDITY:

The cause of most diseases.

HUMOR:

1. I take humor seriously. The essence of humor is contradiction - which just happens to be the essence of everything.
2. The first sweetener invented.
3. Sugar-coated truth.

HUMORLESS:

Someone who suffers from an irony deficiency.

HUMP:

What a camel has and what a lecher does.

HUNCHES:

If you believe in hunches, you really ought to read, *The Fullback Of Notre Dame.*

HUNTING:

1. The war of the weak on the weaker.
2. The knavery of "bravery."
3. There would be nothing wrong with hunting, if the animals had the guns.

Hunting

HURT:

If it doesn't hurt, it doesn't work.

HUSBANDS:

Husbands husband resources which is why wives consider them cheap. And, indeed, if it were left to husbands, the clothing, jewelry, floral, cosmetic, greeting card, and candy industries would all wither on the vine and what a GREAT tragedy that would be! Still, husbands are an essential ingredient in the life plan of the woman who has to have everything.

I

I KNOW WHAT I LIKE:

When did taste become a substitute for knowledge?

IBM:

Used to mean I've Been Moved. Now, with all the terminations, it means I've Been Massacred.

IDEALIST:

A person who believes that people are good, America is the greatest nation that has ever existed, crime does not pay, and women are the weaker sex. In a word, an Idiot.

IDEAS:

1. Having a new idea is not the point; having a good idea, is.
2. I love ideas: They illuminate experience; they do not replace it.

IDEOLOGY:

1. Thought that is for sale.
2. Used to be considered the opposite of Truth until it was determined that Truth was an ideology. Now, it is believed that there is no difference between Truth and Ideology, but that we should be for the former and against the latter, if only we knew how to tell them apart. The Federal Trade Commission is considering improved labels.

IDIOCY:

Marx spoke of "rural idiocy." That may have been characteristic of his time. What is characteristic of our time - when hundreds of millions worldwide have migrated from the country to the city - is urban idiocy. Well, actually, what is characteristic of our time is total idiocy.

IDOLATRY:

1. The finest minds of the 18th Century renounced religion. We have returned to it, only we call it technology.
2. Making excuses for the inexcusable.

IF:

If me no ifs. Tell me when.

ILLEGAL IMMIGRANTS:

Desperate people usually enticed here by avaricious businesses to do the grunge work the citizenry is not willing to perform, for which they are paid sub-minimum wages, while working and living in sub-human conditions. In a word, illegal immigrants contribute nothing, get away with murder, and come here just to take advantage of the Good Life. They should all be sent back to where they came from - but only after they can no longer work, or we no longer need them.

ILLITERACY:

People complain about illiteracy but what about illiterature - *what* people read when they *do* learn to read. The period from the French Revolution to World War I was a time when some great literature reached a mass audience. Since then, a great audience has reached mass shiterature.

ILLTH:

Sickness is painful; health boring. We must learn to endure both.

ILLUMINATION:

Either you illuminate the map or you alter it. The writer does the former; the revolutionary the latter.

ILLUSIONS:

"I have given up all my illusions:" The greatest illusion of all.

IMAGES:

Substitutes for imagination.

IMITATION:

It's pathetic how people imitate themselves. This is the origin of the tic.

IMMIGRATION PROBLEMS:

Started when the Brown, Black, Yellow, and Red people let the White people in.

IMMORALITY:

Saying publicly what you think privately. Exercising freedom instead of exorcising it. Very dangerous.

IMMORTALITY:

1. America is the only country in the world where cryonic suspension (immortality) is for sale - and has found buyers. Available at prices to fit every pocketbook: Fullbody cryonic suspension for you (or your pet) can be purchased for $135,000; whole head suspension (your head is housed appropriately enough in a hatbox) can be had for a mere $40,000; and for the low, low price of $25,000 you can order brain-only suspension. This proves what many have long suspected: Death is Un-American.
2. If you could live forever, at what age would you choose to do so? The most detailed investigation of age and achievement indicated that athletic ability peaked in one's teens or twenties, creativity in one's thirties, leadership in one's fifties and sixties, while popes and supreme court justices got to the top of their game in their eighties and nineties. Moral: If you want to have a long and productive life, become a pope or supreme court justice. But would you want to live forever at age eighty or ninety? Isn't it nice not to have to choose the age you would become immortal? No wonder dying is so popular.
3. The only thing that is immortal is the yearning for immortality.

IMPERIALISM (Late 20th Century):

Gunboat diplomacy has been replaced by helicopter hegemony.

IMPORTANCE:

If you go by how people act, the only things that are important are the things they don't have.

IMPRUDENT MAN DOCTRINE:

Dragging a man out of a burning car, because you have to act and can't think about the possibility that he might sue you later for spraining his shoulder.

INACTIVIST:

People should do less and think more.

INCENSED:

He went to church and smoked pot. Amazing grace or amazing grass- it was all the same to him.

INCEST:

The rape of Mother Earth.

INCOMPATIBILTY:

When the income, tastes, expectations or amusements of one are not compatible with those of the other. Easily remedied if families that stay together would neither pray, pay, or play together.

INCONSISTENCY:

1. Just about the only thing you can count on.
2. If you can juggle three balls in the air at the same time, you're considered clever; if you can keep three ideas in your head at one time, you're considered inconsistent.

INCURABLE DISEASES:

These at least provide the consolation that one needn't bother trying to do anything about them.

INDECISION:

The longer you take to make up your mind, the less necessary it seems to do so. Indecisiveness has the advantage of taking the urgency out of things. Indecision is also less likely to get you into trouble: There is only one way to do nothing, but many ways to do something, from whence it follows that there are more ways to go astray if you act decisively.

INDEPENDENCE:

Independent individuals are aware of public opinion. They just don't share it.

INDIFFERENCE:

It is not a bad thing to be indifferent to things that are indifferent.

INDISPENSABILITY:

Indispensable people are the ones who should have been fired long ago.

IN DISPRAISE OF PRAISE:

Praise is often indistinguishable from flattery, which is why it makes some of us somewhat uncomfortable.

INDIVIDUALISM:

Having the mass media extol individualism is like having Rev. Moon say, "Think for yourself."

INDOOR PLUMBING:

This is the age, par excellence, of vulgarity, noise, ugliness, stupidity, brutality, and speed. Other than indoor plumbing, it has little to recommend it.

INFALLIBILITY:

What we really hate about the doctrine of infallibility is that it is not applied to us.

INFERIORITY COMPLEX:

Discovered by Adler and cured by his Elevator Shoes.

INFORMATION DEVOLUTION:

To be more informed is not necessarily to be better informed.

THE INFORMATION EXPLOSION:

1. When news from somewhere is replaced by noise from everywhere.
2. The information explosion is aptly named, for it is an unmitigated disaster which has left millions of shreds and shards of mind lying about.

THE INFORMATION HIGHWAY:

Where's the exit ramp?

INFORMATION IMPLOSION:

1. A little knowledge is a dangerous thing, but a lot of knowledge is stupefying.
2. The more we know, the less we understand.

INFORMATION OVERLOAD:

1. The anorexic is surrounded by food, but cannot eat. The informationally overloaded are surrounded by facts, but cannot think. "Fact"

itself is not a fact, but a concept. The demand for ever-more facts yields no more understanding than the demand for ever-more food yields satiety. To end hunger, you have to digest and assimilate food; to end ignorance, you have to digest and assimilate facts. "Facts, just facts," is fiction.

2. If "information is power," information overload is paralysis.

INFORMATION RICH:

No day passes that I don't learn of at least ten sordid things that go on in Our Wonderful World that I hadn't known the day before. Ignorance is bliss - probably the only kind left. Lord, keep me ignorant. Information rich is pleasure poor.

INGRATITUDE:

When people are not grateful for being patronized.

INHERITED WEALTH:

When Nelson Rockefeller wished to don his coat, he would throw back his shoulders and throw out his arms knowing that someone would be sure to rush up and put it on him. He did nothing for himself; like royalty, he expected to be served. This is what a baby does. Which is why the really rich are so envied: They can afford to remain babies all their lives.

INNER PEACE:

The way to be at peace with yourself is to recognize that at times you will be at war with yourself; the peaceful co-existence of war and peace is necessary to the well-disordered life.

INNER PERSON:

Speak of the "inner person" these days and people think you're referring to their X-rays.

THE INQUISITOR:

When the Mad Mullah vowed to terminate Salmon Rushdie, he proved that the spirit of the Inquisition lives on...the Torch having merely been passed from one faith (including some that are secular) to another. "Believe as I do or die," happens to be a singularly compelling argument. No wonder it is never given up.

INSANE ASYLUM:

If someone believed he was Alexander Hamilton, he was housed with someone who thought he was Aaron Burr. That would either cure him or kill him. That was more or less the theory behind insane asylums. Today, we de-institutionalize the insane in order to save money, which turns our entire society into an insane asylum.

INSENSITIVITY:

1. It used to be said in defense of insensitivity that you couldn't make an omelet without breaking an egg. Today, we know that you shouldn't eat omelets.
2. Sensitivity is an essential property of life. Those who endeavor to make themselves insensitive to problems - their own and others' - thereby join the serried ranks of the living dead. The "flight to the suburbs," exurbs, and other boobburbs is a flight from fecundity to sterility. To be relieved of life's problems is to be relieved of life.

INSIGHT:

1. Absolutely the last thing in the world a corrupt society needs is insight. We are fortunate indeed to have an institution that *guarantees* we will never achieve it: The educational establishment. Private schools are as successful in avoiding insight as public schools. They differ only in this respect: The private school avoids insight by fetichizing success, the public school avoids it by assuring failure.
2. Sometimes, you have to stop looking at a problem in order to see it: Sight can be a hindrance to insight.

INSOLUBLE:

It's nice not to have to solve problems. The easiest way to do that is to declare them insoluble.

INSOMNIA:

1. One can get too worked up about insomnia. After all, the memorable nights are the ones you haven't slept.
2. Those without sleep are without hope.
3. The problem some people have sleeping is due to the fact that that's what they were doing while awake.

INSTITUTION:

1. The rise of the institution is the decline of the individual.
2. The institution is the tomb of its original purpose.
3. Institutions are instituted as means to accomplish particular ends. Inexorably, the means become the ends - the preservation of the institution becomes an end in itself - *the* end in itself.

INSTRUMENTALISM:

Intellectual life has been reduced to knowing which side your bread is buttered on. People become smarter and smarter at doing what is dumber and dumber.

INSURANCE:

You can never have enough insurance, but you can go broke trying.

INTEGRITY:

The cynical view is that if a person doesn't have much of anything else, he can be said to have integrity...either that, or he hasn't been caught yet...

INTELLIGENCE:

Largely exercised in private gain, has little place in public affairs, which is why, although intelligence can get you to the top, when you arrive there, the view - broad and public - is always disappointing.

INTELLIGENCE TESTS:

1. Invented by people whose intelligence had not been tested. It shows.
2. Supposed to measure intelligence. Although, how you can measure what you can't define has always been a "small" problem.

INTERACTIVE:

When people are given an opportunity to parrot what they heard on the telly.

INTEREST:

Once called "usury," a term of moral opprobrium. After some people made a lot of money from lending money, the practice was no longer deemed offensive and was given the non-judgemental appelation, "interest." If you have to pay it, however, rest assured that though the word has been morally neutered, you will be royally *screwed.*

THE INTERNET:

1. Don't log-on 'till you can talk to God. At the very least, you should be able to communicate with the dead. If you can't do either, enternot Internet.
2. A substitute for intercourse.
3. The mother of all video games.

INTERRACIAL MARRIAGE (The Enlightened View):

But, would you want your daughter to marry one? Sure, as long as he had money.

INTIMACY:

People bewail the loss of intimacy when it is privacy which is endangered.

INTOLERABLE TOLERANCE:

Extreme tolerance leaves one nothing to complain about, which is intolerable.

INTOLERANCE:

People who can't stand injustice are called intolerant.

INUTILITY:

The more a thing costs, the more it is prized. Utility is a secondary consideration, if it is a consideration at all. What is really treasured is pure waste since only someone really important can piss her money away. One differentiates oneself from the herd by ownership and display of what the herd cannot possibly possess and does not need, and, therefore, envies the owner of.

INVASION:

What the enemy does. When we do it, it's called "incursion" - or, if we're having fun - "excursion."

INVENTION:

Necessity may be the mother of invention, but it is also its offspring.

THE INVENTION OF TELEVISION:

When the mind became as superfluous as the vermiform appendix.

INVENTIONS:

Ingenious ways to shorten the time and space between individuals, thereby increasing contagion, confusion, crowding, and copycatting. Inventions also have the inestimable advantage of decreasing privacy, peace and diversity. Is it any wonder that inventors are honored?

INVESTIGATIVE JOURNALISM:

If you've ever read about yourself in the newspaper, or about an enterprise you know, or seen your picture, or noticed how they spell your name, you'll have a pretty reliable measure of exactly how accurate most reporting is.

INVESTIGATIVE REPORTING:

Who's sleeping with whom? Who's on the take from whom? Comment: Who isn't? Who doesn't? Who cares?

INVISIBLE HAND:

The question is not whether we believe in God, but whether She believes in us.

IRONY:

A mask we like to wear because it enables us to be critical without paying a price.

IS THERE A GOD?:

The Deist's answer: Yes, but He doesn't make house-calls anymore.

ISSUES:

Elections are no longer about issues; issues are about elections - who is winning, losing or riding the gravy train.

J

JAPANESE DEMOCRACY:

Participatory paternalism.

JAZZ:

The word comes from 19th Century American slave slang meaning "fuck." The idea that jazz is a legacy of Africa has little foundation. Fundamentally eclectic, jazz has been variously identified or confused with Spirituals, Blues, Improvisations, Ragtime, and Dixieland and has been considered both as a kind of music and a style of performance. For those of us who find that a little of it goes a very long way, it is best described as - boring, which may be why we spell it Gazz.

JEHOVAH, JESUS AND THE JEWS:

Everyone carries a cross or is nailed to one. Jesus is the God of the suffering and Jehovah is the God of wrath. Considering the suffering of the Jews throughout history, Jesus must have been their true Messiah, after all. Since the establishment of the state of Israel, it would seem that Jehovah is more appropriate.

JEWS:

The Spaniards expelled the Jews and Hitler killed them. Spain declined and Hitler fell. The Jews are a most useful people. They can survive everything and be blamed for everything.

JFK ASSASSINATION:

A scab people can't help picking.

JOAN OF ARC:

Doubtless her contemporaries in the church called her Joan of IRK.

JOB-CREATION:

The reason so many new jobs have been created is that where it once took one breadwinner working one job to support an entire family, now it takes two breadwinners four jobs. And the combined income of all the jobs of both people may bring in less real income than the one job of one person yielded in the "bad old days." Now we have more jobs and less money.

JOB DESCRIPTION:

"This job requires a lead bottom, an iron sphincter, a tin ear, a glass eye, a motor mouth, a rhino's skin, and a fat head." This ad was for a job in public relations. How many other jobs does it apply to?

JOB INTERVIEW:

A completely artificial situation in which both sides engage in a competition to see who can lie the best. If an employer wishes to learn the "truth" about a prospective employee, the interview should be conducted in a bar. In vino veritas.

JOGGING:

Sprinting from senility. In the race against time, we know who will win.

JOIE DE VIVRE:

Has been replaced by mal de vivre.

JOKES:

1. The jokes I am interested in are serious jokes.
2. The only way to get away with telling the truth is to present it as a joke.

Jogging

JONESVILLE:

Religions are invented by those seeking to be worshipped. It sure beats working for a living. Besides, there's all that pussy praying to be preyed on.

JOURNALISM:

1. Reporters should never check out all the facts in their stories - they might find that they have no stories.
2. I once heard the editor of a newspaper call the articles in her paper "unpaid filler," which, she pointed out, was far less important than paid filler - advertising.

90

JOURNALISTS:

They don't take sides, they take seats; they are voyeurs not voyagers.

THE JOYS OF TRAVEL:

A contradiction in terms, not unlike painless dentistry. Travel used to be a joy. Now, it's an oy.

JUDAISM:

For some it's Torah-peutic; for some it's Torah-bil.

JUDGEMENT DAY:

The day on which you judge your past and your past judges you.

JUDICIAL ROBING:

Dressing-up to dress-down.

JULY 4th ORATORY:

Air-brushed history.

JURASSIC PARK:

Notable for its special defects.

JURY:

A jury will rarely go wrong if it votes to indict the lawyers.

JUST DESSERTS:

The less we merit something, the more we are convinced of our right to it.

JUST KIDDING:

You remain a kid 'till you have a kid.

JUST SOCIETY:

Entertainers get the money and fame; laborers the contempt and crap. Real work is denigrated; virtual work celebrated. Just? Surely you jest.

JUSTICE:

1. Established injustice.
2. All that exists deserves to perish and, God being just, will.
3. The killers get the publicity; the victims the knife; the lawyers the money.

4. The more horrendous the crime, the easier it is to find a top-flight lawyer to represent you. The publicity alone will make it worth his while to do so, much less the possibility of collecting from the media directly or from what the media pays the defendent for her "story." If you are determined to commit a crime, make sure it is horrible or bizarre enough to achieve bestseller status.

K

KANT:

1. Kant thought that religion was based on morality; his contemporaries thought that morality was based on religion.
2. Kant did not avoid cant. Who Kan?

KARL MARX:

Thought that capitalism leads to war, poverty, famine, homelessness, alienation, crime, monopoly, oligopoly, racism, unemployment, and environmental degradation. History has proven him wrong; we no longer have any of these problems.

"KEEP OFF THE GRASS" SIGNS:

The War on Drugs will try anything.

KEEP SMILING:

And if you detect exhaust fumes, I suppose you'll be told to Keep Smelling.

KEEPING BUSY:

My chief business in life is trying not to keep busy. And I have to tell you that in a world as cluttered and confused as this one, keeping from keeping busy keeps you very busy!

KEEPING FIT:

Keeping fit and keeping young are two separate things, but only the former is possible. So what? You can be young and feeble as easily as you can be old and fit.

Keeping Fit

KEEPING UP WITH *THE NEW YORK TIMES*:

The Times takes too much time to read. But news junkies can't kick the habit. Here's how to solve the dilemma: Read all the stories on the front page, but only the last paragraph on the continuing page. That way you get both the point of the story and the inevitable blunting of that point. *The Times*, being fair, is of course addicted to the "on the one hand…and on the other hand" school of journalism. Beyond that, the Table of Contents on page 2 can be scanned. It shouldn't take more than 10 minutes a day.

KEVORKIAN'S CREED:

Live and let live isn't enough any more. Live and let die is also needed.

KHRUSCHEV:

Swore Russia would catch up with and surpass the U.S. Wherever he is today (we have a pretty good idea) he must be very pleased: Russia *has* caught up with us in slime, crime, and corruption and surpassed us in pollution, inflation, and alcoholism. Indeed, it is *unequalled* among developed nations in one respect: people die younger, on average, than anywhere else and the age of death keeps dropping. Now if *that* isn't progress, I don't know what is!

KILL:

What the bad guys do; when the hunters do it, it's called "cull." It is sometimes said that you can kill with kindness. Few examples leap to mind.

KILLING:

If you do it for God or Country, it's all right. If you do it for a reason, it isn't.

KILT:

You could get kilt wearing one, or you could get kissed. It all depends on what, if anything, you're wearing underneath.

KINDER, GENTLER NATION:

A kinder, gentler nation is one in which no one is fired, but many are excessed; it is a country where there is no unemployment, but there is downsizing; it is a place where you don't cut people, you cut costs.

KING KONG:

Going Ape.

KINGSHIP:

The great thing about being king is that you're not expected to do anything, except show up - and you're accepted for what you are: A figurehead - who expects to be paid in very large figures. It figures, doesn't it? Do less, dough more.

KLAUSTROPHOBIA:

Depression felt by some during the Christmas holidays.

K-9:

If the price is right, you can get people to do anything. But you can't get a dog to wag his tail for any amount of money. No wonder, Schopenhauer preferred dogs.

KNIGHT AND DAY:

In England, persons of extinction are Knighted. In America, this is considered Dayted.

KNOW! KNOW! NO, NO:

To know what to avoid knowing is also to know.

KNOWLEDGE:

Most of what we "know" really isn't so, and the rest isn't important.

KNOWLEDGE ISN'T POWER:

The way things are, even the person who becomes aware of conditions doesn't usually escape their consequences.

KNOWLEDGE, SCHMOLEDGE:

We know that nothing good will happen, yet we keep hoping. . .which proves how little knowledge counts for.

KVETCH:

A person who pisses in the stream and grumbles because the water isn't pure.

L

L.A. RIOTS:

And the Lord said, "Let there be loot!"

LABOR:

Try not to.

LABOR RELATIONS:

There is a fundamental conflict of interest between management and labor. You can paper it over, ignore or deny it, but you won't eliminate it.

LABOR-SAVING DEVICES:

Very useful because they give us more time to complain about how over-worked we are.

LACK OF COMMUNICATION:

The latest all-purpose alibi. It's not the lack of communication that troubles me, but the lack of conversation: When I *don't* want to talk to people, I "communicate" with them.

LADY LUCK:

1. People are envious about the undeserved good luck of the winners of the lottery. But would it be luck if it were deserved?
2. Misery loves lotteries. They are what the desperate use in place of hope.

LAETRILE:

Remember Laetrile? Supposed to be the Answer to Cancer, it was really the pits: Apricot pits.

THE LAFFER CURVE:

I live to laugh; I laugh to live.

LARRY KING LIVE:

Looks more dead than alive.

LATTER-DAY LUDDITE:

Computer refuter.

LATTER-DAY UNCLE TOM:

Beltway Black.

LAUGHTER:

A wonderful substitute for happiness.

LAW AND ORDER:

1. When Chaos is King, the cry goes up for "Law and Order." But the Rule of Law has turned into the Rule of Lawlessness: If you have enough money, power, or pull, you can commit murder and get away with it. If you're poor, you can be hung for minding your own business. It's all a matter of getting the Right Lawyer. The Right Lawyer is defined as the lawyer less interested in being right than in being rich.
2. The criminals that land in jail are the unsuccessful ones. We don't punish crime, we punish failure.

THE LAW OF CONTRACT:

In an expanding universe?

LAW OF GRAVITY:

People who always look serious are just covering their stupidity with gravity.

LAWS:

1. Laws are written by people who know how to avoid them.
2. The rules put in place to protect the privileged few from the under-privileged many. May sometimes be used to ameliorate the lot of the many as long as they do not disestablish the rule of the few.

LAWYERS:

The only lawyers I ever met who actually liked practising law were the ones who didn't have much of a practice.

LAUGHING GAS:

Comical chemical.

LAXATIVE:

When the rich, famous, and powerful are put on trial for their crimes, it acts like a laxative on their stopped-up envy for the masses. And even if the R , F, & P. are acquitted, or merely have their wrists slapped, catharsis occurs and pressure on the social system is temporarily relieved.

LAZINESS:

Let us thank God for laziness. It, along with cowardice, are the two things that save people from wickedness.

LEADERSHIP:

1. The ability to mislead.
2. We are a very fortunate people: The highest offices in the land are held by the craziest people.

LEADERSHIP OR FOLLOWERSHIP GAP:

Great ships need deep harbors.

LEADERSHIT:

Where do our leaders come from? The vast sewage system that is latter-day society backs up and the shit rises to the top.

LEARNING:

1. Anyone can learn if they are desperate enough. Need is the great teacher; want and deprivation are the scourges.
2. If everybody was smart who would flip burgers for a living?
3. Learning is unlearning.

LEARNING FROM LIFE:

What one learns is that people never learn.

THE LEFT:

There's nothing left of the Left. As to the radical press, it has been reduced to shredded bleat.

LEFT OUT:

A major reason why America never developed a serious Left Wing is because of the race problem. So long as there are African-Americans to be despised, blamed and kicked, whites, however poor and alienated, feel themselves privileged.

LEFT-WINGER:

Someone who is for the poor, not *of* the poor.

LEGAL EAGLE:

1. When he can't control the evidence, he discredits its source.
2. He was reputed to have a razor-sharp intellect - meaning that he could slice the baloney real thin.

LEGAL SKILL:

The most important legal skill is procrastination.

LEISURE:

If you're rich, you're "leisured;" if you're poor, you're "lazy." When the King enjoys himself, it's called an idyll; when the beggar enjoys himself, he's called idle.

LESS:

Is more.

THE LESSER EVIL:

1. In politics, the lesser evil is the party out of power. Put it into power and it has the means and opportunity to become the greater evil, which it will, unfailingly, do.

2. The lesser evil is the sapling; the greater evil is the oak. One does not "choose the lesser evil." One merely waits for it to develop.
3. Let us be grateful, not for who won the election, but for who didn't.
4. Forget about lesser or greater, let's talk about good and bad.
5. Don't get discouraged, the country has always survived despite its leaders. The important thing is to be unillusioned, not disillusioned.

LETTERS TO THE EDITOR:

Many men have retired to devote themselves entirely to writing Letters to the Editor; sharing, as it were, their vast knowledge of nothing with the vast world of know-nothings.

LEVITTOWN:

They promised us utopia; they gave us suburbia.

LEX TALIONIS:

If you believe in an eye for an eye and a tooth for a tooth shouldn't you believe that rapists should be raped, wife beaters beaten, torturers tortured, and cannibals eaten?

LIBERATION:

Who will liberate us from it?

LIBERTY:

Liberty does not require law but law requires liberty.

LIE:

Photographs don't lie.

LIES:

1. Lies are to truth what counterfeit coin is to money: As long as you have one, you have the other.
2. Comforting thoughts.
3. People who say they never lie are lying.
4. Anyone who says that everyone is a liar is a liar.

LIFE:

1. Just one damn thing after another - none significant.
2. Life has no meaning, but meaning has life.
3. Life is not a problem to be solved but an experience to be enjoyed. Play it for laughs.
4. Life moves on without paying us any attention. We should try to return the compliment.

LIFE AND DEATH:

1. Life: Vastly over-rated. Death: Vastly under-rated.
2. Life is the mistake that death gives us an opportunity to correct.

LIFE AND DEATH DECISION:

As between life after death and death after life, I prefer the latter.

LIFE EXTENSION:

Medicine used to be about relieving pain and suffering. Now, it seems to be about prolonging them.

LIFETIME UNION:

The advantage of long-lasting marriage is that you don't have to seek someone to argue with.

LIKE:

Like if young people couldn't use the work "like"...like they couldn't say anything...Lacking "like," they'd be out of luck.

LIKING AND LOVING:

If you can like people without loving them, you can love people without liking them.

LIMITS:

There is nothing wrong with accepting one's limits; there is a lot wrong in not trying.

LIMITS OF KNOWLEDGE:

To know is not necessarily to understand. Know-how has little to do with know-what, whether, if...Most of what we know, really isn't so.

LINCOLN REVISED:

You don't have to fool all the people all the time in order to make fools of them most of the time.

LITERACY:

1. Teaching adults who can't read to feel ashamed.
2. Fortunately, I forget most of what I read.

LITERARY CRITICISM:

Fiction about fiction.

LITERATURE:

An elitist word. True democrats and all editors prefer to call it "copy."

LITTLE MAGAZINES:

Writing for them is like sending a message in a bottle: It may never get there (wherever "there" is) and the addressee is unknown and very possibly non-existent. Writing for the Samizdat in post-Khruschev Russia got you a bigger, more responsive audience than writing for Little Magazines in America.

LIVE COVERAGE:

Instant communication has the same relation to truth that instant coffee has to real coffee.

LIVING:

How you make your living needn't have much to do with how you live.

LIVING FAST:

If you live fast, you die young. If you live slow, you wish you were dead.

LIVING SIMPLY:

Living simply is too complicated. It has become simpler to endure the complications.

LOGIC:

1. A little logic goes a long way. The problem is that there's a much longer way yet to go, life being refractory to logic.
2. The victory of logic is always short lived.

THE LONE RANGER:

Not to be trusted because he was a loner. Of course, he had Tonto who could say only one word: "How." As long as The Lone Ranger could add the word "much," it was enough.

LONELINESS:

If you're feeling lonely, see a lot of people by all means. That ought to cure you fast.

LONG LIFE AND HAPPINESS:

But what if they don't go together? The people I know trying hardest to live forever needn't bother. They died intellectually long ago. The happiest people I've met were poor and short-lived. It's easier to loosen up if you're not holding on.

LONGEVITY:

1. If you live long enough, you get to see every single one of your beliefs, ideas, estimates, and theories proven wrong. This is, of course, a privilege reserved for old people who think.
2. Now that we are living longer, we have more time to worry about dying.

LONGING:

People can't unite around programs any more. What unites them is a shared longing for something better than the injustice of a history which has hurled millions into burning ovens. This is the longing that religion was supposed to satisfy, but couldn't and that socialism appealed to before it failed. Nevertheless, the problems remain and with them the longing - thus, the hope.

LOOTING:

If there were never any looting, who would buy theft insurance? For that matter, how could the Police Department's budget increase?

LORD BYRON:

Proved that you can live with a limp, as long as it isn't your dick.

LOSS:

1. It is said that in the last years of his life, Ezra Pound lost his mind. His loss was our gain.
2. If the newspapers all disappeared, we'd have a lot less garbage.

LOSS OF SELF:

How can you lose what you never had?

LOST:

This is a world in which everyone feels lost - because they are lost.

LOT IN LIFE:

Life is a lottery - most of the time you lose.

LOUD:

Loud people shouldn't complain of invasion of privacy.

LOVE:

1. Obsession, fortunately short-lived.
2. The master-slave relationship gift-wrapped.

3. Folie à deux.
4. To be loved for oneself is not what one wants. One wants to be loved in spite of oneself, for one's bad qualities. Only such love is unconditional.
5. Love advances as fear retreats.

Love

LOVE OF LEARNING:

We learn best from those we love best.

LOVE YOUR LOCAL LUDDITE:

I applaud when I see people kicking or cursing a recalcitrant car or computer: Better to abuse a dumb machine than a dumb waiter or animal, a docile mate, or a helpless child. The machine neither feels the abuses, nor cares. Best of all, it's not likely to pull a knife on you.

LOYALTY OATHS:

In the '50's to get a teaching job you were required to sign a loyalty oath. In the '90's you have to answer "correctly" such questions as, "How have you demonstrated your commitment to women's issues in your current position?"…"How do you 'help' your colleagues do so?" Political correctness should no more be required than loyalty oaths.

LULLABYE:

The problem with life is that one spends entirely too much of it awake.

LUST:

1. Compared to chastity, this is the luster of two evils.
2. We should never forget how we got here - through sheer, blind lust.

LYING AND IMAGINATION:

Lying is an exercise in imagination; imagination is an exercise in lying.

LYNCH MERRILL:

Merrill Lynch is bullish on America. Considering how they make their money, they're really bullish on bullshit.

LYNCHING:

The trouble with lynching was that it wasn't done to the right people: If the white-sheeted KKK had hung from the trees, The Fruit of the Limb would have been both more picturesque and more appropriate.

M

MACHIAVELLI REVISITED:

Wealth, a commanding position, inside knowledge - and the ways in which these become reciprocally determined and indivisible remain the real levers of power.

MACHINES:

Americans have a love affair with machines because, up to now, machines haven't claimed their rights. When the new generation of smart machines starts to insist on equal treatment, we may find we don't like them so much, after all.

MADISON AVENUE:

A happy choice of name - since admen are madmen.

THE MAFIA:

According to Hollywood, they control everything: Which means they control Hollywood:

MAKIN' AND BREAKIN':

Lawyers make money two ways: When they write the laws and when they stretch the laws. The big difference between the counselors and the crooks they defend is that legal makin' and breakin' is more profitable and less risky than illegal breakin' and enterin'.

MAKING A WILL:

Splitting heirs.

MALE AND FEMALE:

Male: That portion of the human race that creates all the problems. Female: That portion of the human race that gives birth to and nurtures the other portion of the human race.

Male and Female

MALES:

There are two kinds of males: Those who keep up with their child support payments and those who do not. The first kind is tolerable (we won't say good); the second kind is intolerable (we will say evil). It is politically correct for females to employ male attorneys (themselves probably in arrears) to press delinquent daddies. Thus, males can be useful despite the fact that, unlike females, they suffer from Original Son.

MALTHUSIANISM:

The notion that the supply of people exceeds the supply of food. This doctrine is trotted out every time there is a famine anywhere in the world. When the famine, the people, or media interest die out, things return to normal: Crops are burned, dumped at sea or warehoused 'till they rot in order to keep prices high, while growers are paid ever-larger subsidies *not* to plant. From this we may conclude that the problem is not that the supply of people exceeds the supply of food, but that the supply of greed exceeds the supply of feed.

MANAGEMENT:

1. The successful manager *follows* events closely while claiming to lead them, loudly.
2. Management is like gardening; it has to do with planting and weeding; i.e., hiring and firing.
3. In management, it's less what you do than how you do it.

MANAGEMENT BY DEFAULT:

The best way to get people to do things for you is not to do anything for yourself.

MANAGEMENT THEORIES:

There are no management theories, only management fads.

MANAGING EDITOR.

Jumps when the advertiser so much as farts - then he compliments her on the sweetness of the smell and the balminess of the breeze.

MANICHEISM:

The war between good and evil has been resolved by an agreement between the two parties - to continue fighting 'till one or another triumphs. At which time both will take a short rest before resuming hostilities.

MANIPULATIVE:

Some people have a sense of direction. The manipulator has a sense of indirection. For him, the shortest distance between two points is crooked.

MAN'S BEST FRIEND:

1. It's easier to excuse a dog's bad breath than a friend's bad faith.

Man's Best Friend

2. If you kick your dog, he whines and licks your foot. No wonder he is man's best friend. We love the dog because he is cowardly and servile. In other words, we love him because he is like us, with two redeeming exceptions: He is loyal and he doesn't make inane conversation.

MAPS:

Maps are more helpful than plans.

MARINE RECRUIT:

Fresh flesh.

MARLBORO MAN:

Coughin' all the way to the coffin.

MARQUIS DE SADE:

The analyst who was an analist. In the age of AIDS, he has become, "The Enema of the people."

MARRIAGE I:

1. The chief cause of divorce.
2. It's not what you have in common that counts; it's how well you tolerate what you don't have in common.
3. A matter of give and take: Take a little, give a lot.
4. Marriage is ok; it's monogamy that's the problem.
5. Marriage is a fine institution, but who wants to live in an institution?

Marriage

MARRIAGE II:

If you can't be a member of the oppressing class, at least marry one. Life may not be more satisfying if you do, but it is less insecure.

MARTYRDOM:

Sanctified Suicide.

MARX, KARL:

The outstanding rabbi of the 19th Century. He sought to establish heaven on earth - which was about as likely as heaven in heaven. . .

MARY, MOTHER OF GOD:

The First Unwed Mother. Now do you see the kind of problems illegitimacy can cause?

MASS COMMUNICATION:

The goal of mass communication is mass moronization.

MASS CULTURE:

Maximum audience; minimum meaning.

MASS EDUCATION:

A contradiction in terms.

MASS GUILT:

When all are tainted, none are tainted. Indeed, taint becomes the tint of choice.

THE MASSES:

This term is no longer politically correct. They're now called bottom-feeders.

MASTURBATION:

Infection free ecstasy.

MATERIA MEDICA:

It takes more skill to be a doctor today, but it also takes more patience to be a patient.

MATHEMATIZATION:

The rigor of mathematics is precisely its limitation.

MATURITY:

You know you've reached maturity when you stop trying to make the world a better place in which to live and concentrate on trying to move your bowels regularly.

MAXIM:

The fact that there's a maxim for every occasion is reassuring. It means that your particular problem has been encountered - and countered - before. Familiarity breeds content.

McDONALD'S:

Coffee - very hot; Food - not so hot.

MEANDERING:

To say that streams meander is not to say they are directionless. They go where resistance is least. Management by meander follows the same course.

MEANING:

The mere fact that life has no meaning does not keep us from looking for one. Whose hunger has ever been satisfied by the knowledge that there is nothing to eat?

MEANING OF LIFE:

To get on television.

MEANS AND ENDS:

1. If the end doesn't justify the means, neither do the means justify the end.
2. As reason grows in the means used, unreason grows in the ends those means are used for.

MEDAL:

Palpable pointer of improbable performance.

MEDIA:

Could be a hell of a lot meatier.

MEDICAL CARE:

One good thing about the rising cost of health-care - it's made death more acceptable.

MEDICAL PROGRESS:

The shift from acute to chronic illness, from infectious to degenerative disease, from fast fatality to lingering illness, from the dead to the living dead.

MEDICAL SCIENCE; MEDICAL SAUCE:

If my leg is broken, I see Doctor Boneset; if my heart is broken I see Doctor Chivas.

MEDICINE:

Doctors will tell you that 3/4's of their patients have nothing wrong with them. That is why doctors are able to cure 3/4's of their patients. In general, cures for non-existent ills are extremely successful.

MEDIOCRITY:

The presence of absence.

MEDITATION:

1. The preferred euphemism for indolence.
2. Returning your mind to its natural state: Emptiness.

MEETING THE COMPETITION:

Reducing the American worker to coolie status.

MEETINGS:

Meetings are held not to arrive at a consensus but to arrive, meet, and consent to meet again.

MEGA MERGER:

Heaven and hell are now under the same management - which should tell you what you can expect in the Hereafter.

MEMORIAL DAY:

We should remember the millions who died - for nothing.

MEMORY:

Never regret having a poor memory. What is more efficacious in sparing one regret?

MEN:

Brutal, macho, lewd. No man could possibly understand how a woman feels - ever. Of course, all women understand how a man feels - always: It's very simple - men only want one thing - really.

THE MENTAL HEALTH INDUSTRY:

Quick fixes for every problem; quack problems for every fix.

MERCENARIES:

Their idea of patriotism is loyalty to the first syllable thereof: Pay.

METAPHYSICS:

Why is it that the only questions worth asking are unanswerable?

MICHAEL JACKSON:

Is he the Sheik of shreik or the Sheik of schreck?

MIDDLE CLASS MORALITY:

What does not offend, alarm, or stir people up is considered good. One wonders what Jesus Christ or Socrates, the pre-eminent troublemakers of their times would have made of that. What is truly offensive is not to feel offended in times as offensive as these.

MIDDLE MANAGEMENT:

Since it's always in the middle, it can barely manage, which is why middle management tends to be muddle management.

MIDDLE MANAGER:

Spends his life flattering the fatheads above him and fooling the fatheads below him.

MILLENNIAL MUSING:

If Christ returned today and saw what the church has become, his first words would be, "I am not a Christian."

MILLENNIUM:

Miller Time.

THE MINISTRY:

A minister shouldn't have a church, he should have a calling. Give him a church and he becomes a caretaker of property, not souls. Christ's message lives despite the church, not because of it.

MIRACLE:

1. A selfless deed done anonymously that confers no tax or other material advantage.
2. Who says science doesn't believe in miracles? Consider how much money is spent monitoring the radio spectrum for extraterrestrial signals.

MIRACLES:

The most miraculous thing about miracles is that people believe in them.

MISANTHROPIC MUSINGS:

We hear a great deal about the problems of the Homeless. What we don't hear is that homelessness can also be a solution. Think of the things the Homeless *avoid:* Junk mail; bills; taxes; faxes; unwelcome calls; nagging relatives; badgering bankers, salesmen, repairmen and insurance agents; mortgage payments; shoveling snow in winter; mowing lawns in summer; painting, fixing, cleaning; World Wide Web waits. Ah, the Happy Homeless!

MISDEEDS:

We love to hear about the misdeeds of the mighty because they make our misdeeds seem trivial.

MISFORTUNE:

More easily borne, if we take heed of The Great Truth that to suffer misfortune you first must have the good fortune to be alive.

THE MISS AMERICA CONTEST:

Corn with your Porn offering the ultimate in lookalike, soundalike, peekaboob prizes.

MISS CONGENIALITY:

Congenial people don't care what they say as long as it is comforting. It's hard to be honest *and* congenial.

MISSED OPPORTUNITIES:

When I think - really think - of the missed opportunities in my life, I figure I haven't missed much.

MISSIONARIES:

1. First they fell on their knees, then on the aborigines.
2. Many a missionary was a shill for a mill trying to sell cloth to naked savages pulling the wool over their pudendas, as it were.

MISTAKE:

1. The biggest mistake is the fear of making a mistake. Looking for India, Columbus found America; searching for spice, the Portuguese found gold.
2. Generally speaking, old mistakes are corrected by new mistakes.

MISTAKES:

1. We are told to learn from our mistakes. What we learn is to make other mistakes. This means that in order to keep learning we have to keep making mistakes.
2. We don't learn from our mistakes, we learn to make them undetected.

MISTER:

The word Mister is a corruption of the word Master. Both words are now politically incorrect. The politically correct salutation is Monster.

MISTRUST:

Mistrustful people mistrust themselves. They spend entirely too much time answering objections no one raised.

MISUNDERSTANDING:

The statement regarded with deepest suspicion in the Age of Depth Psychology is the direct statement. Since Freud, everyone tries to find out what people "really" mean. Causation has been replaced by motivation. What is most obvious is now least obvious, as "deep thinkers" spend more time looking at what is not there than in looking at what is. We forget that the difference between appearance and essence may be nonsense.

MODERATION:

Philosophers praise moderation but rarely practice it. After all, philosophy means *love* of wisdom - and when was love of anything ever moderate?

MODERN ART:

1. Shock and schlock.
2. It gets your attention, but it doesn't keep it.

MODERN CLASSICAL MUSIC:

Unsound.

MODERN MEDICINE:

Heroic measures in medicine produce reverse Darwinism: Survival of the Unfittest.

MODERN POETRY:

Fashionably thin books that are unread except possibly by three relatives, two dependents, and another would-be bard. They are always favorably reviewed - by poets, of course, (who else could possibly appreciate them?) who understandably expect the same favor when their thin tomes are released. This conveniently closed circle constitutes a marvelous mutual admiration society which hews to a unique principle: Any book of poetry that actually sells is *prima facie* suspect. Why are so many published if so few are bought? T'is the insanity of vanity.

MODESTY:

1. Almost extinct instinct in an age when not to scream and yell is not to buy and sell.
2. A modest person is someone who doesn't burst into the house boasting to his wife that he didn't have an affair today.

MOLTING POT:

Tho' Americans pride themselves on having absorbed hordes of immigrants in the past, they feel threatened and overwhelmed by immigrants in the present. None are less tolerant than the sons and daughters of recent immigrants - busy migrating from a past they are still ashamed of.

MOM AND POP STORE LAMENT:

Is there life after Wal-Mart?

MONA LISA'S SMILE:

There's nothing mysterious about it: She'd just broken wind.

MONARCHY:

When kings of old led their troops into battle and were somewhat exposed to the dangers they inflicted on others, life seemed fairer than it does in our own democratic days, when battles are ordered by commanders-in-chief who never come near the fields upon which they order others to die.

MONEY:

1. Always run it down, but make absolutely certain that you get as much as you can.
2. It's not work that makes money it's money that makes money. Fundamentally, you have two career choices: To work or to make money. If you want to make serious money, you major in money and go where it is. What you don't do is work for a living. In a word, it's more lucrative to be a broker, banker, bookie, or shirker than a worker.

MONOGAMY:

To love only one is selfish.

MONOTHEISM:

An attempt to establish a monopoly. Ordinarily, this sort of thing is challenged by the Justice Department on anti-trust grounds. In this instance, they can't be trusted to do their job. I believe in deodiversity - preferring to disbelieve in several Gods, not just One.

MONOTOTHEISM:

The notion that there is but one God.

MORAL MINIMALISM:

I make no claims for the way I live my life beyond the fact that it suits me. I do what I have to do in the only way I can get it done. For the rest,

I try to do as little harm as possible, recognizing that in a world as screwed up as this one is, and given my limited knowledge and power, there is no way I can avoid doing some harm.

MORAL OF THE STORY:

Few of those who preach or teach morality practice it.

MORAL REGRESSION:

Man is unique among the animals in knowing the good and doing the bad. So, if you tell me knowledge is power, I answer: So what? Indeed, if our knowledge of good and thus, our capacity for it, increases, but our moral condition remains the same, progression is regression.

MORALISTS:

Moralists are often people so busy saving civilization they have ceased to be civil.

MORALITY:

To feel solidarity with struggling, suffering human beings and animals, and to wish to link one's fate in some measure to theirs, at least to the extent of trying to alleviate and/or eliminate some of their pain is what morality is about. If, as Schopenhauer thought, the foundation of morals is compassion, there is little reason to be surprised that our time is so lacking in morals.

MORE:

Is less.

MORMONISM:

What happens when you let the genealogy out of the bottle.

MOST FAVORED NATION:

Procrastination.

MOST MOVIES:

They move; you are unmoved.

MOTEL SIGN:

"You are always welcome here. Have a good lay."

MOTHER RUSSIA:

The choice seems to be between dictatorship and anarchy. The majority choose Vodka.

MOTHERS:

My mother used to say: "Make sure you wear your rubbers." Now, doctors say: "Make sure you wear your condoms." (See: Mothers Do Know Best.)

MOTION SICKNESS:

The computer is more attractive than the book to some because words move on the screen but not on the page. What matters most in the age of the motion picture is motion.

MOTIVE FOR MASTURBATION:

Familiarity breeds...

MOVIE THEATRES:

The real money in movie theatres is made by the candy concession which is very fitting: The body and the mind both need to be filled with junk.

MTV:

The flight into light, movement, and noise designed to render thought impossible and the viewer deaf, dumb, stunned, and stoned. The same thing used to be achieved by the House of Horrors at the circus, only now on TV the circus runs non-stop. Is it any wonder that so many members of the younger generation are deaf, desensitized, inarticulate and illiterate?

MUCKRAKING:

Classical muckraking exposed social scams: Holding companies, trusts, monopolies, the stranglehold of the oil industry, etc. Modern Muckraking deals with the sex life of the Rich and Fatuous. *Its* object is to make the private parts public and the public parts private.

MUDDYING THE WHITEWATERS:

The beauty of having D'Amato investigate BiHillary is that Honest Al could never be accused of inexpertness in impropriety.

MUMMIFICATION:

The ancient Egyptian ruling class spent vast sums of money to achieve immortality through mummification. 18th Century English business-men decided that pulverized mummies made superior fertilizer. So thousands of mummies were ground up, shipped and sold round the world. Moral of the story: The belief in immortality is a bunch of shit.

MURDER:

What would Hollywood do without it? And what would happen to the criminal justice system or the small arms industry if it went out of style? For that matter, what would all the people do who now write Letters to the Editor, "viewing it with alarm?" How fortunate we are that we don't have to worry about the disappearance of this grand old custom. Murder may be the only way to bring comfort to the truly resentful.

MURDOCH, RUPERT:

The mass murderer of good taste. On hearing that he had acquired Harper Collins, a writer was heard to say: "The only book he ever read was a checkbook."

MURK:

Many ideas are simple, clear, coherent, rational, logical - and wrong. Impenetrability and obscurity also have their rights. Don't smirk at murk.

MUSEUM:

A place where it's posh to nosh, shop and stop, pick up greeting cards, calendars, or wrapping paper - and, who knows, maybe there'll even be time to look at a picture.

MUSEUMS:

Used to be refuges: Quiet, empty, tomb-like. Now, they swarm with people taking tours and pictures. The guards all have walkie-talkies; you stand in line to get in and once there, you stand in line again to see the pictures and you better look fast and keep moving at blockbuster exhibits. You pay admission or make a "donation," the amount of which is "suggested," so that if you don't give at all or don't give "enough" you feel as guilty as though you'd sneaked in. Then, there are the gift stores, selling T-shirts, bumper stickers, cups, toys, and reproductions and the restaurants *and* fast-food feedlots. Museums have become upscale malls. Like department stores, they justify their existence in terms of numbers - attending and contributing; they don't just exhibit anymore, they sell - themselves, their shows, their wares, and the curators' personalities. Their latest wrinkle is to rent themselves out for weddings, parties, anniversaries, and Bar Mitzvahs. Once you could go to a museum, not only to look, but to dream. The dream is over.

MUSIC HISTORY:

From Mostly Mozart to Mostly Muzac.

MUSICAL CHAIRS:

As mental hospitals are emptied, prisons are filled. "Safe streets" are not necessarily sane streets.

MY FAIR LADY:

"Why can't a woman be more like a man?," ran the refrain of one of the songs in this hit musical. How times have changed! Written today, the line would surely be: "Why can't a man be more like a woman?"

MY POSITION ON NUTRITION:

It's zinc or swim.

THE MYSTERIOUS EAST:

Bangkok - where the inscrutable becomes the unbreathable.

MYSTERY:

What is incomprehensible is the fact that the universe is incomprehensible.

N

NAIVE:

Those who possess defective shit detectors.

NAMES:

In America, everything from planes to hurricanes are given names; we personalize things and de-personalize people.

NANNY:

Rising young feminist executives who want it "all" (babies *and* careers) *now* need nannies - preferably stupid, strong, foreign females unfamiliar with such neologisms as "minimum wage," "social security," "benefits," etc. (They have no "need to know" and "wouldn't understand" or be "interested" in such arcane and boring details, anyway.) How does the flourishing feminist reconcile her feminism with the exploitation of her less-fortunate sisters? The same way slave-owners quieted their consciences: By saying, "Half-wits only need half-a-loaf."

NARCISSISM:

Eye to I.

NARROW-MINDED:

Someone who suffers from a protean deficiency.

NATION:

Nations are not superior to one another. Some are simply better at hiding the truth about themselves than others.

NATIONAL BOOK AWARD:

The Good Housekeeping Seal of Approval for mid-list masterpieces that good housekeepers can feel good about reading.

THE NATIONAL INTEREST:

Every politician talks about the national interest while serving his own interest.

NATIONAL SECURITY AGENCY:

The particular peculiarity of the parasites who work here is paranoia.

NATURAL:

1. The worship of the "natural" is unnatural: It is human nature to alter nature.
2. No one knows what this word means anymore, so everyone prostrates themselves before it...naturally.

NATURALISM:

A literary school specializing in forgery.

NECESSARY EVIL:

If it's necessary, it's not evil and if it's evil, it's not necesssary.

NECESSITY:

There's a lot to be said for it - where there's no choice, there's no anxiety.

NEIGHBORHOOD CHURCH:

Our Lady of Perpetual Bingo.

NEO-AGE:

We are no longer in the New Age; we are in the Neo-Age: Neo-Conservatives; Neo-Liberals; Neo-Fascists; Neo-Nazis. Why neo? No one wants to be pigeon-holed, labeled, or seen as pre-packaged. When a politician calls himself "neo," he means: "Take any position *you* like. Remove from it all the parts that offend *you* - I'm what remains."

Although neo means new, it's now used to mean quasi - which is why you can be driven quasi, trying to figure out what it "really" means.

NERO:

Another victim of poor P. R. It is not true that Nero fiddled while Rome burned. In actuality he piddled...he was trying to put out the fires using only "natural" methods.

NETWORKING:

Society and the family are not working. In their places we have networking.

NEVER GIVE UP:

People who never give up, by definition, never get what they want.

NEW:

If it's new, it's not important. If it's important, it's not new.

NEW AGE SEW-AGE:

1. Granted we are all dying of thirst in the desert of contemporary life, but does that mean we *have to* drink from a stream that is only a mirage?
2. A "New Age" is proclaimed, on average, every three months.

NEW AGE THERAPIES:

Laughing, crying, tickling, stroking, pinching, pounding, and recreational farting. Once, one did these things naturally. Now, they have been elevated to the level of "remedies."

NEW AND IMPROVED:

1. Costs more than it used to.
2. Same old shit with a different name.

THE NEW CLASS:

We now have pet-loss support groups, pet-grief hotlines, pet funerals, memorial parks, and psychologists. Since the number of singles doubles every couple of years, we can expect more and more pets to inherit substantial fortunes. Will this create a new petit bourgeosie?

NEW EXCUSE:

Considering how many selves I contain, it's a real pain in the ass having to choose which one to wear every morning...that's why I'm late...

THE NEW PARADIGM:

The new paradigm is that there is no new paradigm. Indeed, there is no paradigm. Instead of paradigms, there are only fads. This is, doubtless, an example of paradigm lost.

NEW PHYSICS:

Whatever is - isn't.

THE NEW POLITICS:

The Reagan Revolution reversed 50 years of political rhetoric. Before him, poverty was considered a condition to be remedied not reviled. Roosevelt claimed to be waging a war on the haves; Johnson, a war on poverty. Reagan taught politicians that they could get votes by enriching the rich while waging war *on* the poor. Clinton's rhetoric neither glorifies the rich nor vilifies the poor; it focuses entirely on the middle class. As for outcomes, his policies are largely a continuation of Reagan-Bush by other means: The rich get richer and fewer relative to the whole; the poor poorer and more numerous, and the middle class continues to dwindle and descend. Where will it all end? Why do people think there has to be an end?

NEW VIEW:

It used to be important to see ourselves as others saw us. It is now important to see ourselves as a TV camera sees us.

NEW YEAR'S RESOLUTION:

Not Nietzsche's "live dangerously," but Ariosto's "live resolutely." As for me, I live fitfully.

NEW YORK CITY:

"I wouldn't want to live there." Believe me they don't want you. They've got enough complainers already.

NEW YORK CITY GOVERNMENT:

To govern it one needs a firm hand, deep sensitivity, a willingness to listen, charity, compassion, an unending supply of State and Federal aid, the complete support of the business, banking, bond-brokering, and criminal community, the cooperation of labor, The Cardinal and the Gays, plus compliance by the Jewish, Italian, Irish, Black, Hispanic, Chinese and Japanese communities, in addition to a working knowledge of Russian, Hebrew, Arabic, Yiddish, Italian, Japanese, Chinese, and Korean. In a word, New York City is ungovernable. Not to worry. That's the secret of its survival.

THE NEWS:

1. Too important to ignore; too trivial to recall.
2. Whatever is on TV at 6:30 P.M. It doesn't have to be new. In fact, it never is.

NEWSPAPER HEADLINES:

Used to be called "screamers."

NEWSPAPERS:

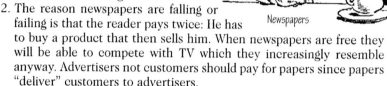

Newspapers

1. I never read them. I prefer being uninformed to being misinformed.
2. The reason newspapers are falling or failing is that the reader pays twice: He has to buy a product that then sells him. When newspapers are free they will be able to compete with TV which they increasingly resemble anyway. Advertisers not customers should pay for papers since papers "deliver" customers to advertisers.
3. They're called newspapers, but the amount of space available for news is determined by the amount left over from advertising, the comics, the horoscope, advice to the lovelorn and hypochondriacs, and cute pictures.
4. Newspapers won't help you understand anything, but they will help you talk about it.
5. Balance in newspapers means giving equal weight to the true and the false.
6. Newspapers need to be called something else - if it's new it's on TV; if it's in the newspapers, it's no longer new. We can't very well call them "oldspapers" and it's not accurate to call them "truespapers." We could call them "notsonewspapers" or "toiletpapers" since that's where they're often read and what they often are.

NICE:

We are never more apt to be dishonest than when we are being "nice."

NIGHTMARES:

Used to be experienced only at night, but now that we are again living in The Dark Ages, they can also be seen throughout the day.

NIKE:

A major engineering feet.

1980'S:

When the scum floated to the top.

NIXON:

Rasputin revisited - you had to be a genius to be that devious.

NIXON FUNERAL EULOGIES:

Listening to all the flattering crap that was said about him made you wonder if there aren't an awful lot of people who think the only good politician is a dead one.

NO OFFENSE:

The old can offend without inhibition. Unfortunately, by the time they're old, they're no longer interested.

"NO PROBLEM":

When I was in Poland, I found people who didn't even know English using this phrase. What it really means when people say, "No problem" is that they are having one hell of a problem, but they'll be damned if they'll admit it to you.

NO SMOKING?:

Shouldn't dying persons have a right to smoke? Should pregnant women have a right to smoke?

NOAM CHOMSKY:

Beacons are useful to those whose eyes are open.

NOBILITY:

We go to the theatre and are deeply moved by some noble words. On the drive home, the uplifting feeling is slowly diffused by the attention we have to pay to traffic. By the time we arrive tired, what was an experience has become a memory. The following day, we are already planning our next outing. Nobility has been replaced by mobility.

NOMINEE (Presidential):

The choice is always treated as though it were a big surprise, although everyone knew months earlier who the nominee would be (usually the one who extracted the most cash to spend on the race from the vested interests), "dark horses" having been relegated to the dustbin of history, or what is worse, to the vice-presidential nomination.

NON-CONFORMITY:

Out-of-season fruits are always welcome. If you are not different, you are not.

NON-DISCRIMINATION:

Being nice to everyone proves you lack discrimination.

NON-FICTION:

Not to read fiction is like dressing without a mirror.

NON-VIOLENT PROTEST:

A useful tactic rather than an absolute principle. Turn the other cheek if you must, but at least fart.

NONSENSE:

The Sixth Sense...although in respect to frequency of use, it is undoubtedly the first.

NORM:

Don't worry about being unhappy. It's normal.

NORMAL:

A normal person is someone who has not yet visited a psychiatrist.

NOSTRILS:

Are always "flaring," as breasts are always "heaving," horsehoofs always "thundering," and crowds always "clamoring."

NOTHING:

When nothing can be done, nothing should be done. What you avoid can be as important as what you accomplish. A void to the wise is sufficient.

NOTRE DUMB:

When the French gave Sylvester Stallone and Jerry Lewis the Legion of Honor.

NOVEL:

The name should be changed if they don't have anything new to say.

NOVEL THOUGHT:

People who don't read novels claim they have "better things" to do with their time - like looking down on people who do read novels.

NOVELLA:

A novel for women.

NRA:

Nuts R Armed.

NUCLEAR ENERGY:

One of the Seven Blunders of the World. Probably tops the list.

NUDITY:

As far as being erotic is concerned, nudity is only skin-deep. In a nudist colony, nudity is not obscene. It is, in fact, too much seen, which has led some people to define obscene as the less-seen. As in politics, a little cover-up helps.

Nudity

NUREMBURG TRIALS:

Victor's justice.

NURSING HOME INMATES:

Either their minds are gone and their bodies are good, or their bodies are good and their minds are gone.

NUTRITIONAL ANALYSIS OF THE CANDIDATES:

Clinton: High fat, low (moral) fiber; Dole: Acid reflux.

O

OBLIGATIONS:

We no longer have obligations, only options.

OEDIPUS:

What makes Oedipus timeless is that the hunter was also the prey. Oedipus is the classic example of how we are our own worst enemies.

OF FOOLISH THINGS:

"If fifty million people say a foolish thing, it is still a foolish thing."

OFF THE RECORD:

Many problems would disappear if they weren't talked about.

OFFENSIVE:

If you didn't offend some people, you'd never get rid of them.

OFFICE-HOLDER:

The Army's slogan is, "Be all that you can be." The officer-holder's slogan is, "Get all that you can get."

O.J. SIMPSON:

We've always known you can get away with murder if you're white, rich, and powerful, and that if you're poor, black, and male you can be murdered by the state just for looking at a white female. If O.J. was guilty of murder and walked, a partial revolution in civil rights would have occurred: A black male got away with murdering two(!!) whites, one of them female yet (!!!). Of course, a black man can only do this if he is Rich and Famous: Rich, because he can afford the Right Lawyer (which see), and famous because all the media attention ostensibly makes "a fair trial impossible." The civil rights struggle has certainly taken some strange turns when Murder, Inc. becomes an equal opportunity employer.

OKRA:

Mucilaginous muck;
Tastes like Yuck.
Cooked with mumbo-jumbo,
Makes a tasty gumbo.

OLD AGE:

1. The greatest killer of all...more people die of this than anything else.
2. The great blessing of old age is that one can, at long last, indulge in that contempt for the opinions of others that alone brings a modicum of intellectual satisfaction.

OLD DOGS:

What I like about old dogs is that their needs are simple, their loyalty boundless, and they sleep 20 hours a day.

OLD FART:

Not a pejorative; "Old Fart" is a purely descriptive phrase, unfortunately.

THE OLD MERCHANT'S DREAM:

To be able to run a thriving business without customers - or just a few, who are a pleasure to talk to, to whom one can sell just a few choice items, at fair prices, without bullshit. Auf jener welt.

OLIVER NORTH:

I've seen pianos that are more upright and Grundyites who are less uptight

-OLOGY:

The simple addition of these five letters converts any activity into a science; e.g., cosmetology.

ON REACHING AGE 67:

When I grew up every town had its A&P. As I grow older, every day has its A&P: Aches and Pains. *These* are the "best days?" Give me a break. "Golden Ager." Either an oxymoron or just a plain moron. But I am easily satisfied:

All I ask -
To be free of pain
And still able
To complain.

ON TIME:

1. Being on time has achieved the status of a moral imperative. But, the executioner is always on time. Isn't the important thing what you are on time for?
2. Those who are always on time waste a lot of time being on time.

ONE'S FIRST SEXUAL EXPERIENCE:

Always a disaster, unless committed with a sympathetic, older friend or relative - in which case it was "child abuse."

ON LANDING THE CONTRACT TO BUILD THE STEALTH BOMBER:

Wealth by stealth.

OPEN COVENANTS, OPENLY ARRIVED AT:

These are usually the covenants not worth covering up.

OPINION:

In a formal democracy such as ours, opinion rules, but what rules opinion are the ruling opinions; i.e., the opinions of rulers or, if you prefer, the opinions of the establishment.

OPPORTUNITY:

1. The difference between innocence and guilt is opportunity.
2. "There are no problems, only opportunities." Translation: You don't solve problems, you make money out of them. Opportunity is for opportunists.

OPPRESSION:

Only among oppressed people do ideas still matter.

OPTIMISM (For Pessimists):

1. I have nothing against optimism, but in America it has assumed the proportions of a major epidemic.
2. An optimist is someone who *may* think that life is wonderful but *must* think that about death.
3. As long as most things still go wrong, there's a chance they can go right. Pessimists only get really worried about the future when everything goes according to plan and there are no surprises.

ORIGINAL SIN:

The establishment of orthodoxy.

ORIGINALITY:

Over-rated. We'd be much better off if we didn't strive for it and behaved as though something had been learned in the last 5,000 years.

ORPHANAGES:

Institutions for the poor are almost always poor institutions.

ORTHODOX JEW:

"I'm very tolerant - some of my best friends are Christians."

OSCARS:

The best example of equal opportunity. No film is ever bad enough to be unable to win some award.

OTHER PEOPLE'S CHILDREN:

Always perfect. Hold them up as an example to your child: "Why can't you be like little Ronald? *He* never picked his nose in public and stuck the yuck under the seat..."

OUGHT:

What should be points to the falsity of what is.

OUTING AS AGAINST STAYING IN THE CLOSET:

When the right to be deviant clashes with the fun of being devious.

OVAL BALLOONS:

Leaks from the Oval Office are usually trial balloons. If successful, the leaks become lakes.

OVER 85'S:

Said to be the fastest growing segment of the population. Lots of best-seller possibilties in this. How does this title grab you: *The Power To Deflower at 85?*

OVERHEARD IN THE LADIES ROOM:

"The hell with his I.Q. - what's his sperm count?"

OWNERSHIP:

Ownership is O.K. as long as no one owns you.

OY:

What you get when you take the "j" out of "joy."

P

PAIN:

1. The most powerful stimulant.
2. You don't need to feel pain to feel pained.
3. People are so constructed that there is nothing plain, even about pain. Thus, there are some individuals for whom pain is a source of plea-sure, especially if it is experienced by others. When someone begins a conversation with, "It pains me to say this," what they really mean is, "It gives me pleasure to say this."
4. Few things give greater pain than the realization that others enjoy pleasures denied to us; few things give greater pleasure than the real-ization that we enjoy pleasures denied to others.
5. But even if pain is a pain, only the dead don't feel it.
6. Don't complain about pain. Past a certain age there is little else left to keep us interested.

PAIN IN THE ASS (PITA):

People who complain of pain in order to give pain are a real pain.

PAINT BY NUMBER:

Advertising statistics.

PAPERWORK REDUCTION ACT:

It reduced neither paper nor work; it reduced their *rate* of increase, thereby justifying continued increase.

PARADIGM:

There's many a paradigm not worth a dime, much less twenty cents. SEE "Twenty Cents."

PARADIGM SHIFT:

Government *was* the enemy; business *is* the enemy.

PARADISE:

Unhooking a bra.

PARENT-CHILD RELATIONS:

If they're independent, they don't need you; if they're dependent, they never let you alone.

PARKS AND WRECKREATION:

Pity the public park: What no one owns, all despoil

PARTICIPATORY MANAGEMENT:

When leaders follow their followers.

PART-TIME JOB:

God only works one day a week. No wonder the world is in such poor shape.

PARTY:

When the likes of Perot want to start a Third Party, you know it's time to stop partying. Either that, or you start a Fourth Party.

PAT BUCHANAN:

A blindman shooting at a target all day will hit it once or twice - which doesn't make him either a marksman or a seer.

PAT ROBERTSON:

A man of the cloth - cashmere. Would that the soul business were his sole business.

PATHOLOGY:

Where you end up depends on what happens along the way. In economic theory, this is called Path Dependence. It should have been called Pathology. Under either name, it underscores the significant role in human affairs of accident or, as it is sometimes called, circumstance.

PATRIOTISM:

Why is patriotism like prostatitis? Both share a feeling for nation - although in the latter case it is urination.

PATRIOTS:

On July 4th, patriots celebrate revolution; every other day of the year they seek to destroy it.

PBS:

Public Begging System.

PBS COMEDY SHOW:

The McLaughlin Report.

PEACE IN OUR TIME:

Conflict manifested in forms that conceal conflict.

THE PEACEABLE KINGDOM:

The lion and the lamb will lie down together - provided that they are suitably sedated.

PEDAGOGICAL PROGRESS:

In the 19th Century, preachers molded souls; in the 20th Century, teachers mold souls; in the 21st Century, media and machines will mold souls. By the 22nd Century, machines will have souls and souls will be machines.

PEDESTRIAN:

Since so few people walk any longer, there is nothing pedestrian about being a pedestrian. It is the automobile which has become pedestrian.

PENIS:

Mons best friend.

PENIS ENVY:

The real reason Lorena liberated her husband's member.

PEOPLE:

I've always preferred God's people to His principles - except when I prefer His principles to His people.

PEOPLE'S CHOICE:

In the voting booth, some voters use *the eeny, meeny, miny, moe* method and others, *the he loves me, he loves me not* system. There's as little to choose between the methods as between the candidates.

THE PERFECT MARRIAGE:

The perfect marriage is one in which two people are perfectly content not to be perfectly content.

THE PERFECT WAGNERITE:

Wagner set Hegel to music.

Perfect Marriage

PERFECTION:

1. Right can be put into things, but things can never be put right.
2. Perfection does not depend on duration or magnitude: A circle is a circle whether it is large or small; happiness is happiness whether long or short-lived.

PERISH THE THOUGHT:

The only thing that may save the planet is the extinction of the human species.

PEROT SUPPORTER:

Only intelligent people could be that stupid.

PERSEVERENCE:

Keep sailing even though there is no land in sight and the prediction is for poor weather.

PERSONAL SECRETARY:

Everybody needs a pit bull.

PERSONALIZATION:

Don't "personalize" your letter; write personal letters. There's nothing more de-personalizing than personalized letters.

PERSONNEL MANAGEMENT:

Some people make mistakes and some people are mistakes.

PERSONNEL PROBLEM:

1. Given his record as troublemaker, if Jesus came back today, he couldn't get a job.
2. Even God had to put up with a revolt by the angels.

PERSPECTIVES:

1. When you've grown up, teenage pregnancy is the problem; when you're a teenager, teenage abstinence is the problem.
2. To keep your illusions, keep your distance.

PERSUASION:

Wanting to make other people share your opinions is, after a certain point soon reached, absolutely indecent. We have entirely too much persuasion and entirely too little conversation.

PERVERT:

The name given by the inhibited to the uninhibited.

PESSIMIST:

1. The person who has noticed that people act better when things are worse.
2. For the pessimist, worst-case analysis is first-case analysis.
3. An optimist says, "Things could be worse;" a pessimist says, "They will be."
4. A charter member of the Frequent Flayer's Club.

PESSIMISTIC VIEW:

Too good to be true; too true to be good.

PETS:

Who else is petted and feted, tho' their breath be fetid?

Ph.D:

1. The doctoral dissertation combines impressive incomprehensibility with imposing insignificance.
2. It's much easier to become a Ph.D if you have a Ph.G (Papa Hut Gelt).

PHALLIC WORSHIP:

Now considered a phallacy.

PHILANTHROPY:

1. The alms industry.
2. If there were no tax collectors there would be no philanthropy.
3. Aid no longer goes to the needy but to the greedy. If you examine who the recipients of both the charitable dollars and federal grants or loans are, you discover the same thing: The recipients of the largest part of the largesse are those who already have. It is not the poorest countries, projects, people, or institutions that get the bulk of the money, but the safest, wealthiest, and best-connected.

PHILOSOPHER AND FOOL:

The philosopher doubts everything and regrets nothing; the fool regrets everything and doubts nothing.

PHILOSOPHY:

1. A 2,500 year-old conversation in which everything is discussed and nothing is decided.
2. Philosophy is the love of wisdom, not its attainment.

PHLEBITIS:

Caused by the bite of a phlea:

> Approach the phlea -
> It will flee.
> It is trying
> To be free
> To bite you,
> To bite me.

PHONINESS:

In a phony world mostly phonies make it to the top. If you weren't a phony when you climbed up, you'll become a phony after you arrive.

PHOTOGRAPHY:

1. A method for preserving moments we were once lucky enough to forget.
2. Photography became popular when it was realized that photographs were preferable to the people photographed.

PHYSICIAN-ASSISTED SUICIDE:

Don't ask, don't tell.

PIE-IN-THE-SKY:

At least it's not fattening.

PILLORY:

What's being done to Hillary. It's enough to make Bill bawl and Chelsea crawl.

PITY:

1. How can you feel pity for individuals who *choose* driving over drinking?
2. The problem with pity is that if you feel it you're not supposed to show it; and if you show it, people doubt you feel it.
3. Feeling sorry for someone for not being as wonderful as you.
4. One is sometimes overwhelmed with a feeling of pity for poor people: They seem so vulnerable and gullible. Then one notices how they treat each other and the feeling passes.

PIZZA HUT:

Our boys fought and died to make the world safe for Pizza Hut.

PLAGIARISM:

How bad can it be? If someone plagiarized my work, I would view it as the tribute paid by discrimination to genius.

PLANE FARES:

The only things that go up faster than the planes.

PLANNING:

1. We spend 3/4's of our lives planning what we never do and doing what we never planned.
2. I enjoy planning. You expect me to take it seriously, too?
3. When plans work out, it only means that we are stuck with our mistakes.

PLANT LIFE:

There are people who talk to plants. Big deal. I talk to the wall.

PLASTIC SURGERY:

1. A very poor substitute for what is really needed by most of the individuals who seek it: Brain surgery.
2. The designer vagina followed hard on the erection injection.

PLATITUDE:

What is oft-repeated. So oft, in fact, that it makes us repeat. A platitude deserves little gratitude; it wastes our time and lessens our latitude.

PLAUSIBLE DENIABILITY:

Doing what the boss wanted, although he never said in no uncertain terms that he wanted it done, so that you can't say in certain terms that he did not want it done. Got that? In other words: If it fails you're blamed; if it succeeds he's praised.

PLAY AND PLEASURE:

The only worthwhile things. Heed the happy hedonist: Duty's for the dumb. "Do as thou wilt" was the rule in the House of Theleme. The rule should be that there are no rules.

PLAY THERAPY:

The debasement of play to the level of function.

PLEADING GUILTY:

1. Has little or nothing to do with *being* guilty.
2. When the State pleads with the accused to say that he is guilty of a lesser offense, so that it does not have the expense and trouble of feeding, clothing, and housing him. Guilt and innocence, crime and punishment, have less to do with weighing evidence on the scales of justice than they have to do with balancing the books.

POETRY:

Nobody reads poetry any longer. That's why it's a Good Thing.

POLICE:

Impossible to police.

POLICY WONK:

Someone who makes it a policy to get everything wronk.

POLITELY CONNECT:

Connected is respected; the elect connect. The more messages you get, the more important you are and the less you get done, which also testifies to your importance - the main thing being to network, not work.

POLITELY CORRECT:

"I have never had the pleasure of meeting her," is what is said; "I have had the pleasure of never meeting her," is what is meant.

POLITICAL:

So what did you expect? After all, read from right to left it is "Lacitilop."

134

POLITICAL ANATOMY:

Gladhanding; asskissing; backbiting; backscratching; fingering; palming; brainwashing; and ball busting.

POLITICAL CHANGE:

There are three kinds of political change:
1. Name change.
2. Title change.
3. Small change.

POLITICIANS:

1. What they promise is reform; what they bring is change. But while reform requires change, change does not require reform.
2. Politicians promise people things they can't, won't, or shouldn't provide.

POLITICS:

1. The manipulation of fools by knaves.
2. The art of the passable. The question isn't if it's possible, but if it's passable.
3. Bargaining, or if you prefer, trading.

Politics

POLLS:

1. Ask a stupid question and you get a stupid answer.
2. A scientific sampling of unscientific prejudice.
3. Asking the ignorant about the obscure to determine the inane.
4. You can get public opinion to come out on any side of any question depending on how you ask it. Ostensibly, polls are conducted to find out what people think, which begs at least five questions: Do people think? Will they tell you what they think - or will they tell you what they think you want to hear - or what they think you think they should think? Is what people think of any interest or value? Do people know enough or are they provided with enough information to have matter to think on? Will what people think matter in terms of what is actually done? The real reasons polls are conducted are (in order of importance): To enrich pollsters (hucksters of the half-baked); to provide the media with something to fill the time and space they have available, in order that adjacent time and space may be sold to advertisers; to make movers and shakers, as well as media mavens, *look* democratic; i.e., look as though they really cared what the public thought. Polls influence policy far less than policy influences polls. But poll outcomes do influence the choice of cliches that politicians use.

POLYGAMY:

Because the Mormons didn't believe in adultery, they practiced polygamy. We practice hypocrisy.

THE POOR:

Since we will always have them with us, there is little point in being concerned about them, say the conservatives. If people want to be poor says Newt, let them be poor. It's called "Laissez-Poore."

POP PSYCHOLOGISTS:

People too busy trying to figure out your motives to listen to your reasons or too busy listening to your "tone" to hear your tune.

POPULARITY:

1. If you want to be popular, it helps to be an idiot. Of course, if that's what you want, you probably are an idiot.
2. Popularity is to worth as pennies are to hundred dollar bills.
3. It doesn't take much to be popular and if you are much, you won't be.

POPULATION PROBLEM:

1. I refuse to worry about this: We are, after all, members of a species with a unique gift for self-destruction, which, one way or another, should eventually take care of the problem.
2. Liberals unfairly criticize the West for doing so little about population control in the Third World. After all, most of the aid given consists of weapons that enable people there to kill one another.

POPULISM:

Once referred to politicians who served the people or at least claimed to. Populism, in our time, means someone who is popular, never mind that he serves himself and his handlers. Reagan was the perfect populist for our time.

PORNOGRAPHY:

A verbal rather than herbal aphrodisiac.

THE PORTABLE PENIS:

Lorena Bobbitt invented this handy convenience which has proven to be an absolute godsend to the busy female executive who must travel frequently. Now, she can just stuff it in her handbag to use when needed without the inconvenience of having to schlep the rest of him. Should also save on telephone bills since the P.P. is a great communicator: At least with it you know what's coming.

PORTABLE PHONE:

You no longer have to be wired to be wired.

POSSIBILITY:

I don't believe in hope, I believe in possibility. The odds are easier to figure.

POST-ELECTION HONEYMOON:

Immediate inflation for the purpose of subsequent deflation.

POST-INDUSTRIAL SOCIETY:

The replacement of production by seduction.

POSTER CHILD:

1. The needy fronting for the greedy.
2. The cute and appealing fronting for the acutely unappealing.

POSTERIOR VIEW:

If posterity will think of me what I think of my ancestors, I'm glad I won't be around to hear it.

POVERTY:

Poor people are nice. That's their problem. Their other problem is that it costs a lot to be poor.

POWER OF NEGATIVE THINKING:

They all talk about the "need to know." It's the need to "no" that's really required: The need to say no to the shit that keeps getting piled on.

PRACTICAL WISDOM:

Practical people are practically always boring.

PRAGMATISM:

After the Red regime succeeded in quelling the protest in Tiananmen Square, the West rushed in to trade with China. Scoundrels and heroes are not judged by their acts, but by their fate.

PRAGMATIST:

It's very impolite to call a politician an opportunist. Call him a pragmatist instead and watch him glow. The point is: A pragmatist *is* an opportunist. (Shh, don't tell him.)

PRAISE:

Praise is not always praiseworthy - what people admire in others is often what they think they have in themselves.

PRAISE OF APHORISM:

The more's the pithy.

PRAVDA:

The truth shall make you free. Really? Isn't it more apt to make you crazy?

PRAXIS:

The "in" way to spell "practice."

PRAYER:

1. May God protect me from being rich, famous, powerful, good-looking, thin, or long-lived. See, God listens.
2. Lord, save me from the the salesmen of salvation.
3. Can you be considered humble if you believe God listens to you?

Prayer

PREDICTIONS:

1. Predictions are fine, but I wouldn't use them to foretell the future.
2. The only thing one can predict with certainty is that "prophets" will be making wrong predictions for the predictable future.

PREDICTIONS OF THINGS TO COME:

When cars come equipped with latrines, drive-by shootings will be replaced by drive-by shittings.

PRE-FABRICATED IDEAS:

Slogans and sound-bites are fed us pre-chewed. We would not dream of swallowing food already masticated. Yet, we think nothing of swallowing its intellectual equivalent, so little is thinking valued.

PREJUDICE:

No method frees us from prejudice. It comes to us in our mother's milk. But, if one is open to counter-prejudice, there is hope.

PRE-NUPTIAL AGREEMENT:

1. Puts finance back into romance.
2. The prudent (wo)man doctrine.
3. Takes the risk out of the risque.

PRESCRIPTION:

1. Early to bed and early to rise means having to listen to fewer lies.
2. The best way to avoid getting depressed is to stay unhappy.

THE PRESIDENCY:

You have to be crazy to want the job. That explains it.

THE PRESIDENT:

1. In America, anyone can grow up to be President. That's the problem.
2. The most powerless man in the world. No wonder: He has more advisors than a horse has flies or a dog fleas.

PRESIDENTIAL POLITICS:

Dollar Bill was not replaced by Duller Bob. Apparently, the electorate prefers spiced baloney.

THE PRESS:

Freedom of the press belongs to those rich enough to own the press. People may need the truth; the question remains whether they want it.

PREY TELL:

Zoos are places where predatory animals no longer prey on each other having become prey to human curiosity.

PRIDE:

Repairs as many damages to the ego as it causes.

THE PRIESTHOOD:

An excellent career choice if your goal is pederasty.

PRIMATE:

That the highest office in the Church of England is occupied by a primate is dramatic proof of evolution.

PRIMITIVE IDEAS:

Primitives don't want their pictures snapped because they believe their souls are being taken; would-be celebrities would sell their souls to have their pictures taken. Who is more primitive?

PRINCE CHARLES:

The only throne he may ever sit on is a Kohler.

PRINCIPLE:

1. "It's a matter of principle:" When you can't think of reasons, you can always fall back on principles.
2. When you're being stubborn for no good reason, stubbornness becomes the reason.

PRINCIPLES:

1. It's one thing to fight for principles, quite another to live up to them.
2. One can be a prisoner of principles as easily as one can be a prisoner of their lack. In all too many cases, people don't have principles, principles have people.

PRINTING:

The second greatest invention ever. Circulated more lies than anything until The Internet.

PRISON:

It may be true that stone walls do not a prison make, but they sure help.

PRISON POPULATION:

The principal reason you find so many Blacks and Hispanics in prison in the U.S. is very simple: The biggest crime in America is to be poor.

PRISONS:

It costs more to keep a person in prison than to send her to Harvard. That's why so many people go to prison: Who wouldn't want an expensive education that is free? The local jail is the Poor Boy's Harvard.

PRIVATE DETECTIVE:

It's a great time to be a private eye: All the lawyers need voyeurs. You can't win a case, if they're not on the chase. When people complain the U.S. has too many lawyers, they forget we have too many prisoners, prisons, police - private and public - judges, guards, criminals, and "crimes." They also forget that crime and punishment is the chief theme of the entertainment media. We are obsessed by crime. What the fuck is wrong with us?

PRIVATE PROPERTY:

The Holiest of Holies. Nothing is more sacred than this - except when they want to put a highway through your property. Then you discover what is even more holy: Economic Development - the greater good having become the greater greed for greater speed.

PRIVATIZATION:

1. Making people pay to use services and things they already paid for with their taxes.
2. Communism talked about the "withering" away of the state and capitalism is trying to achieve it - under the rubric of privatization. This Thatcheristic Brave New World has given fresh meaning to the word "freedom:" Freedom from those who cannot pay; freedom for those who can.

PRIVATIZING:

Subsidizing business.

PROBABILITY:

The one thing we know for sure is that we don't know very much. That being so, what we know is only probably so which means that probability itself is no more than probable. And then there is always the problem of how you calculate the probability of what you don't even know exists, but which, if it does, probably affects the probability of other probabilities.

PROBABILITY THEORY:

A thing's desirability is in inverse relation to its probability. The fact that people crave the improbable is an essential part of gambling's appeal. Compulsive gamblers don't play the odds; they play against the odds.

PROBLEM PEOPLE:

1. Are there any other kind?
2. What I generally do about problem people is the same as what I generally do about minefields - I walk around them.

PROBLEM-SALVING:

Don't think - drink.

PROBLEMS:

Solutions to problems grow clearer the further you are from them.

PROBLEMS OF THE RICH:

It's tough to be rich: If you try to be "one of the boys," people accuse you of being a phony. If you keep apart, they say you're stuck-up. How lucky the rest of us are.

PROCEDURE:

Just because procedures don't work, doesn't mean they make no sense. No procedure, improperly applied, will work.

PROCRASTINATION:

If you let problems pile up, most of them solve themselves. The rest rot and can be recycled.

PROCTOLOGY:

One of the most eminent practitioners in the field is named Dr. Goldfinger. So help me. I couldn't make that up.

PROFESSIONAL CREDENTIALS:

Legitimated larceny; certificated incertitude.

PROFESSIONAL FOOTBALL:

If you ain't cheatin', you ain't tryin'.

PROFESSIONAL SPORTS:

When game becomes gain.

PROFUNDITY:

Profoundly superficial people are superficially profound

PROGRESS:

1. The idea that things are getting better. So what? People aren't.
2. If what most persons call progress is progress, I'm against it.
3. What can we do to stop it?
4. Nobody knows what progress is but the word continues to be used. It doesn't matter. Words have been liberated from meanings and now go their separate ways.
5. No one believes in progress anymore, but everyone is resigned to it.
6. The replacement of pills by gelcaps.
7. Things haven't gotten better, there are just more of them. Thus, for example, World Wars have been replaced by Civil Wars, Police Actions, Interdictions, Incursions, Preventive Strikes, Religious Wars, Terrorism, and "Peace Processes."
8. Progress is a meat-grinder - you put a cow in one end and hamburgers come out the other.
9. Progress consists of undoing what has been done.
10. Humanity keeps advancing; the problem is that goals retreat.
11. In the Stone Age, men wielded clubs; today, they drop bombs; then, they dug holes with a stick; now, they use dynamite; then, they

142

climbed trees if they wanted to look around; now, they rocket off into space. Basically, people do the same stupid stuff; what has changed is that they now make more noise and dirt doing them.

PROHIBITION:

From inhibition to prohibition is a very short step...backward.

PROMISE:

Deferred disappointment.

PROMOTION:

If you want to be promoted, you have to show promise; then development; finally, maturity. Then you're excessed.

PROPERTY:

Proudhon thought that property was theft. The earth was there before man. How a few people could come to own it and the vast majority of people be dispossessed of it could, he felt, only be satisfactorily explained by theft. Our entire civilization, so-called, is built on this "original sin," so deftly committed that its fruit had been miraculously transformed into that Holiest of Holies, Private Property - a sacred shrine at whose base we worship. Since all property is robbery of the many by the few, all rule is minority rule established and maintained, in the final analysis, by chicanery and force. If you do not understand this, said Proudhon, you will never understand anything - which, all things considered, may be the best thing for your peace of mind.

PROPHECY:

If you enjoy lying but insist on getting away with it - for now - try prophecy as a career. You can get lots of respect and make plenty of money, but eventually you will have to change your address and maybe even your name. That's a prophecy. Here are two more:
1. The stupider the proposal, the more likely it is to be funded;
2. Now that everyone has decided that world wars are obsolete, we're bound to have one.

PROSPERITY:

Really big money is made by plundering the past and mortgaging the future.

PROSTATE PROBLEM:

To pee or not to pee.

PROSTITUTION:

1. The world's oldest profession. Unfortunately, many of its practitioners look like they were around when it got started.
2. Love for another lights up parts of oneself, hitherto dark. In love, it is impossible to be unaffected by the other's personality, habits, feelings traits, attitudes, etc. A purely sexual relationship, by contrast, has the advantage (and the disadvantage) that other parts of the self are left relatively untouched. Prostitution may be the world's oldest profession precisely because of its limitations.
3. In San Francisco, prostitutes are called "sex workers." Unlike other workers always on the go, sex workers are always on the come.

PROTECTING THE ENVIRONMENT:

A euphemism for protecting the business environment. Dan Quayle may have been the first, but he was surely not the last, to call environmentalists Communists - which hasn't kept major polluters from calling themselves environmentalists, thereby contributing to the pollution of language.

PROZAC:

1. Steroids for the business Olympics.
2. One of the wonder dregs.

PRUDENCE:

1. Kicking those already down
2. All will be well if you submit, conform, avoid problems, and mind your own business. This is the "truth" taught over and over again by experience. There is only one problem: You will be bored to tears by the living death that unrelenting prudence requires. The answer lies in prudence with the utmost scorn for prudence.

PRUNES:

You know someone is old when they order prunes for breakfast. That isn't all you know about them.

PSYCHOANALYSIS:

1. The sickness it purports to cure.
2. You talk; he listens.
3. The Revised Standard Version of the Confessional.
4. Answers few; theories many.

PSYCHOLOGY:

Psychology isn't science, it's religion that sounds like science.

PTL:

It used to be that ignorance was bliss. Now they've even taken that away: The media have made it harder to avoid knowing. But even if you can't be ignorant, thank God you can still be stupid.

PUBLIC BROADCASTING:

1. Commercial free, but with a fee: Never ending Beggary.
2. Most of the "creative thinking" in public broadcasting goes into determining the best way to raise private money.

PUBLIC EDUCATION:

Public education was never supposed to teach the child to think. It was supposed to teach the child to obey. Nowadays, it does neither which is why the privatization of education is touted. Privatization won't educate or socialize either, but it will prove profitable for some of its purveyors which is, at the end of the day, all that really counts.

PUBLIC ENEMY NUMBER ONE:

Public opinion.

PUBLIC LIBRARIES:

Day care centers for the homeless.

PUBLIC OPINION:

1. I used to worry about what people think. Then I learned they didn't.
2. Public opinion is not the opinion of the public. It is whatever the propagandists and hucksters program it to be.

PUBLIC RELATIONS:

1. In days of yore, it was something you did when you were in trouble; now you're in trouble if you don't do it. Clearly the P.R. people are doing a good P.R. job on their clients. The funny thing is that the clients don't believe the stuff, but are convinced other people do. In this respect, p.r. is like advertising. The new "achievement" of public relations is that it is getting to be unrecognizable: News largely consisting of self-serving P.R. handouts is doctored to look like investigative reporting.
2. The fact that so many people are so poorly off even though there's more than enough for everyone is what makes public relations necessary.
3. Public relations is a euphemism for propaganda.

PUBLIC SERVANT:

It sounds servile, even quaint; yet, one who truly serves the public should not feel demeaned - especially as compared to others who serve only themselves.

PUBLISH OR PERISH:

1. When the Unabomber said he'd stop killing people if the *New York Times* or *Washington Post* printed his essay, he provided us with the last word on publish or perish.
2. Being published doesn't make your stuff good; being unpublished, doesn't make it bad. The real test is whether *you* can *still* stand to read it five years after you wrote it.

PUBLISHING:

1. The bookkeepers have taken publishing away from the keepers of the book and publishing has become grublishing.
2. Used to be about literature, now the books are about crooks, except for the cookbooks, which offer recipes for everything except cooked books. For those recipes, you have to go back to the bookkeepers.

PUNSTER:

Shakespeare was the Pontiff of pun...no one spun a pun like Will.

PURITANS:

No one has a dirtier mind than a puritan. Who else but the impure would make ideological purity an ideal?

PUTTING A MAN IN SPACE:

When this became the priority, the space race became the space ruse. In any event, for political reasons, it'll probably be a woman.

Q

QUALITY OF LIFE:

Insofar as Q.O.L. is concerned, the only thing worse than a declining economy is a booming economy.

QUALITY TIME:

A euphemism for less time. Nowadays, parents give things to children instead of time.

QUANDARY:

If we succeed in eradicating the bad, who will save us from the good?

THE QUIET LIFE:

If you are looking for a quiet life, don't enter a cloister, monastery, or university. Become a Maytag repairman.

QUIXOTIC:

The Don took that very short step from the sublime to the ridiculous. At once sad and funny, noble and foolish, he lived in the world as it should be, not as it was. Since only a hair separates the Quixotic from the Heroic, our feelings about him are ambiguous. Who, after all, is entirely a realist? Who can bear to be?

QUORUM:

The bad thing about lacking a quorum is that you can't even pass a motion to adjourn; the good thing is that you don't have to.

R

R:

Whether people are fiends or fRiends depends on who they R.

RABBI KAHANE:

Genghis Kahane to his "friends."

RABELAIS:

The deepest thinker; the greatest laugher.

RADICAL:

A radical likes to get to the root of things. When she does, she finds dirt.

RADICAL RESTRUCTURING:

Former university radicals are now in control of many departments, top administrative posts and much money; *they* now make the decisions of whom to hire, fire, promote, "restructure out," give or deny tenure; how much money to ask for what and whom; what and how to teach; what and what not to research. The results are neither reassuring nor startling: The old radicals have become the new conservatives; the New Left has become the New Right; heterodoxy has become orthodoxy; the pedants now sport jeans with their tweeds; "thought control" is replaced by "politically correct" and you can be charged with sexual harrassment for *looking* at a lady.

RAGGED INDIVIDUALISM:

A single individual can't change the course of history any longer, but history does change the individual. Rugged individualism has become ragged individualism.

RAINY DAY REFLECTION:

Either the world works imperfectly or we understand it imperfectly. Either way (or both ways), imperfection is all we've got and all we're going to get. At least you don't have to strive for it.

RAISON D'ETRE:

If you need a reason for living, you're already in trouble.

READING:

1. You don't learn to read by reading to learn - you learn to read by loving to read. Reading is, first, an act of love. The way you become motivated to read is by being read to by someone you love, who loves you. Today, kids are *told* to read. They have no reading role models: Their parents are "too busy" watching TV, and/or making more money or themselves more "beautiful."
2. If reading between the lines is good, reading between the words is better.

READING NOVELS:

The 19th Century's drug of choice.

THE REAGAN YEARS:

1. The days of swine and grossness.
2. Greater greed as higher good.

REAGANSPEAK:

"It's morning again in America." Mourning was more like it.

REAL:

When Hegel wrote that only the real is rational and only the rational is real, he was trying to show how far we were from both.

REAL RICHES:

The interior life takes precedence over the exterior. The latter is the means, the former the end. And it is the interior which should measure the adequacy of the exterior. Obviously, the interior world is affected (infected?) from the beginning by the exterior. All the more reason to keep the wound as clean as possible. This order of priority accounts for the persistence of Platonism.

THE REAL STUFF:

It's as much the problems we avoid as the things we accomplish that shows if we've got "the real stuff."

REALITY:

The illusion we are accustomed to.

REBEL:

To rebel much is to be disappointed often; to never rebel is to be a disappointment.

RECURRING ERRORS:

When errors reappear it means that the needs that first brought them into existence have also reappeared.

RECYCLING:

1. Used to be called thrift. Since thrift is unthinkable in a consumer society which survives on the basis of unlimited growth, recycling had to be invented. It doesn't work any better than thrift.
2. Recycling of ideas seems to be more successful than recycling of garbage.

REDFORD, ROBERT:

Romances the pantses off maiden auntses.

REDISTRIBUTION OF THE WEALTH:

In contemporary society, this means shifting money from the poor and middle-class to the rich.

REDUNDANCY:

A euphemism for unemployment. However, there are many employed who are redundant and many unemployed who aren't. It is not necessary to be employed to be useful; it is not necessary to be useful to be employed. What a revolution it would be if instead of worrying about unemployment, we were concerned with useful employment.

RE-ENGINEERING:

Adding unnecessary gimmicks, usually referred to as "bells and whistles," to a product in order to justify a price hike. "Improvements" have long ceased to be options and as many are added as the producer can get away with.

REFERENCES:

References are always favorable, else why would they be offered? Besides one can be sued for saying things that are unfavorable. So, what are you complaining about? You said you liked people to be positive.

REGRET:

What I regret is the time wasted on regret.

REGRETS:

I had hoped to give up hope but found it a hopeless task. . .as hopeless as giving up regret, I regret to say.

REINVENTING:

While Al Gore was busy "reinventing government," Bill Clinton was busy reinventing himself - into a RepubliCrat.

REJECTION DEJECTION:

There's nothing like a publisher's rejection for taking the conceit out of you.

REJECTION SLIP RECIPIENT:

Another victim of the Literary Industrial Complex.

RELAPSE INTO BARBARISM:

In the '60's, conservatives descried hippies for refusing to have their hair cut, considering this a relapse into barbarism. After a while, conservatives began to *hope* for a relapse into BARBERism.

RELATIVES:

Blood may be thicker than water, but no one is thicker than one's relatives.

RELATIVITY:

The relativity of knowledge is precisely what gives it value for the understanding of a reality which is itself relative. Former truths were not necessarily formerly untrue.

RELIGION:

1. Once religion was the opium of the people; now opium (and its derivatives) is the religion of the people.
2. If God really loved man, would He have created him?
3. If we *are* created in God's image, God help Him!

4. Religion today, for the cultivated person, is a cynical belief in a belief in which one cannot believe.
5. Religion is like a fungus - once you've got it, it's very hard to get rid of.
6. Religion is for those who prefer consolation to clarity.
7. Because a thing is devoid of reality doesn't make it devoid of utility.

RELIGIOUS ESTABLISHMENT:

When religion becomes prosperous, prosperity becomes religion.

THE RELIGIOUS RIGHT:

Hate thy neighbor.

REMEDIAL EDUCATION:

Used to mean making things easier; now it means making easier things; in a word, adulteration and diminution. Instead of making the best more easily available, it cheapens, lessens and reduces it or offers "simplified" substitutes. Instead of reading the classics, read digests. Or see movies. What gets remedied by remedial education is effort - both by teacher and student. Should be called ersatz education.

REMEDIAL READING:

Teaching kids who are busy shooting people, drugs, and sperm to spell. A sure sell.

RENAISSANCE:

If late 14th Century Florence gave us the Renaissance, late 20th Century America has given us the Ruinaissance.

RENUNCIATION:

Renunciation is useful because it helps preserve non-material values which might disappear if it disappeared. The good is good, not because it is victorious, but because it resists victory and doesn't insist on unconditional surrender. Good people are not usually successful people. They are more apt to be a rebuke to success.

REPENTANCE:

Forgetting works as well as repenting and is a lot less painful.

REPRESSED:

The name given by those devoid of common sense to those who exhibit it.

REPRESSION:

Everything and everyone that exists bears, in some way, the marks of a repression which is the basis of civilization. Freud knew this but considered it inescapable. Marcuse, on the other hand, distinguished between repression, which he too considered inescapable, and what he called "surplus repression," which he considered terrible precisely because it went beyond what was strictly necessary. This is a distinction that needs to be preserved.

REPUBLICAN FORM OF GOVERNMENT:

The replacement of royalty by royalties.

REPUBLICANS:

1. Not all scoundrels are Republicans, but all Republicans are scoundrels.
2. Altruistic Republicans are as commonplace as speeding turtles.

REPUTATION:

1. Once it was said that all a person had was her reputation. No longer. Now, the best repute is the most repute and the most repute is ill-repute.
2. Promise little; perform much.

REQUIEM FOR ENVIRONMENTALISM:

Environmentalism was supposed to be the issue that cut across class lines. Another illusion. The rich and powerful will always be able to afford a move to a cleaner (even if not a clean) environment.

RESEARCH:

1. Isn't research wonderful? It can prove the truth of either side of any question.
2. Whenever I hear the word used on TV, my guard goes up: "Ah, lies are about to be trotted out in their scientific Sunday suit best."

RESEARCH GRANTS:

Once grants were offered for the purpose of making research possible, now research is for the purpose of making grants possible.

RESEARCH INTO RESEARCH:

The first question to ask about research is: Who paid for it?

RESENTMENT:

Resentments can fuel revolution. In the case of radical feminism, they appear to have replaced it.

RESIGNATION:

I'm resigned to enjoying life.

RESPECTIBILITY:

One's position may require one to be respectable - than which nothing is more boring. Respectability is a heavy tombstone laid over the living dead. If you must be respectable in public, at least be disrespectable in private.

RESPONSIBILITY:

Establishing responsibility is a delicate matter - and even at its best, imprecise and tenuous. What choices were available? Were they presented clearly, or at all? What conditions confronted people at the times and in the places they had choices, if any? Were the alternatives real or imaginary? What might the consequences have been of choosing those alternatives? We are far less free than we imagine ourselves to be or than we are told we are. We accommodate, by and large, to circumstances we neither created, were consulted about, or could substantially alter if we wished.

REST EASY:

Extremes meet: Too much rest results in muscle atrophy; so does too little. I rest my case - and my carcass.

RESULTS:

In our society, everything is judged by results. The difficulty is that results are not judged by everything. "Side effects," long-term effects, and effects on society as a whole, are not part of the results *that count.* Hence, *they* are not measured. We don't count what "doesn't count" and then assume that if it isn't counted, it doesn't exist.

RESUME:

A list of all the places that have put up with an employee and all the places the employee has put up with. Resumes may tell you something about endurance. They tell you little about performance.

RESURRECTION:

Tertullian said of the Resurrection, "It is certain because it is impossible." But it is certainty which is impossible.

RETIREMENT:

1. If in doubt, don't. I'd rather work at work than work at home. The real choice is where you work, not whether you work.

2. Why would one want freedom *from* work if one has freedom *in* work?
3. When will I retire? I retire every night....been doing it for years...
4. If one size does not fit all, why should it be expected that one retirement age fits all? For me, retirement would represent a move from public service to domestic service.
5. The best place to retire? Six feet under.

RETREAT:

It is now very trendy for people to go on retreat - I would have thought it wiser to retreat from people.

REUNION:

It's nice to get together with old friends you haven't seen in years. Just so long as it's years 'till you see them again.

REVEALING:

If something (dress or document) is described as revealing, the question is: Does it reveal the real?

REVELATION:

A revelation only comes when you are ready for it. It was always there; you weren't.

REVERENCE FOR LIFE:

If a fly bites you, swat it. As long as you use a fly swatter and not a swat team, you're displaying reverence. Reverence for life, after all, includes reverence for your own life. You don't have to turn the other cheek to act ethically. Self-defense and proportionate response are reasonable, hence ethical.

REVERSE GESTALT:

The whole can also be *less* than the sum of its parts; the urge to merge of business in the '80's provided many examples of reverse gestalt: Insurance firms that screwed up in the software business; steel companies that tried to sell electronics; department stores that fouled up as stock brokers, etc. The result: The development of a new and lucrative business that consisted in breaking up ill-considered mega-mergers and selling off the pieces. Like they say: United we fall; divided we stand.

REVIEWS:

Useful to those who prefer talking about books to reading them.

REVOLUTION:

1. Another revolving door.
2. If there is to be a new revolution, it will have to come from a new place. Nations are only capable of one major revolution in their history.
3. Revolutions are influenced by ideas, not made by them.

REVOLUTIONARY CAREER:

The struggling revolutionary fights with the police; the successful revolutionary calls them in.

THE RICH:

1. Rich people seem to think money is the cure for all evils when it's the cause of most of them.
2. Rich people will share everything with you except their money.

RIDICULOUS:

The fear of appearing ridiculous is ridiculous.

RIGHT AND WRONG:

1. Knowing the difference between right and wrong is a matter of believing, not knowing.
2. We may not know what is right, but we always know what is wrong.

RIGHT AS VAIN:

If we loved ourselves more, we'd need other people's love less.

THE RIGHT LAWYER:

The lawyer less interested in being right than in being rich.

THE RIGHT TO BEAR ARMS:

1. A license to kill.
2. Given enough time and change of circumstance, everything turns into its opposite. The right to bear arms is a perfect example of how right *becomes* wrong.
3. I prefer bare arms.

RIGHT-TO-DIE:

An issue that is full of life.

THE RIGHT-TO-LIFE:

1. For the true believer, the right to life confers a right to take life.
2. Right-to-Lifers would vote for a tailor's dummy, if it wore a pro-life badge.

RIGHT TO LIFE AND DEATH:

Did anyone ask the sperm or the egg about the proposed merger? Since the decision in favor of creation was made (wittingly or not) by the parents, why shouldn't *they* be the ones to make the decision to terminate?

RIGHT WAY:

There's no "right way" to live; there's only a way that's right for you.

RIGHT-WING TERRORISM:

The democratic impulse replaced by the demoniac impulse.

RIGHTS:

1. Allow people to do wrong.
2. Every right was once deemed a wrong. What made the right right was struggle. Rights that are given can be taken. Rights that are won are less easily lost.
3. Rights are wrested, not "inherent:" The wresting of right is about the only meaning history has.
4. Only animals, children, and the mentally challenged are given rights.

RIGHTS CULTURE:

We live in a time when everyone asserts "rights" - whose number expand daily. What of the right to be spared all this righteousness? Rights don't right wrongs; they regulate them.

RIOT:

Caused by two things - a disturbance of the peace and unrestrained revelry. This proves once again that nothing is more disturbing to the peace of some individuals than the sight of other persons having fun. People are a riot.

RISK:

You jump in the ocean, you get wet.

RITUALIZED PROTEST:

The police are now trained in the handling of protestors, and the protestors are trained in the handling of police. Marches are carefully orchestrated and each side knows in advance exactly what the other will do, how far things will go and how long they will last. From Bolsheviki to Bolshoi ballet in only a few decades.

ROCK MUSIC:

Rock is a crock - monotonous, predictable, dreary - the anvil chorus produced by commingling the sounds of shekels and schrecklicke shreiking. The appeal of rock is the appeal of the pseudo-rebellion - screaming, yelling, and pounding as surrogates for the failed revolution of the '60's. . .sound and fury signifying nothing except the shrill sound of cash registers ringing up ever more and bigger sales.

ROCK STAR:

Spastic contortionist, tortuously twisting and turning in antic Tantric. Concert musicians perform like rock stars while rock stars are "in concert." The name of the (music) game is fame, and, in its name, taste becomes fair game.

ROMANY RIP-OF:

It's very easy to feel for the gypsies - until one of them robs you. Worse than losing your wallet, is losing your idealism.

ROPE TRICK:

When you try to tie up *all* the loose ends you just get more entangled.

ROTTING OF THE MORAL FIBER:

Caused by excess humidity.

ROYALTY:

Royalty

Kick kings out one door, they re-enter through another. America's Republicanism has bred a different kind of royalty - the royalty of entertainers. In Europe, they were merely jesters and jugglers to the monarch, his acrobats, clowns, musicians, and performers. In America, this motley crew is richer than the royalty it once served! Hollywood, TV, the music industry, and the playing fields are where you make the money and get the kind of fame, adulation, and loyalty once accorded only to kings. Moreover, our entertainers live by a set of rules separate from those imposed on the rest of us. Indeed, they are expected to do so, exactly as the monarchs once did. Meanwhile, in Great Britain, the "Royals" survive *because* they are a source of entertainment for the masses and stories for the media. The Lord moves in mysterious ways, his democratic miracles to perform. Kings ruled by divine right; basketball players rule by divine height!

RULE FOR REVOLUTIONARIES:

Remain resolute. You are living on ideas yet to be understood, much less realized.

RULE FOR WRITERS:

Writers should write not in order to be understood, but to understand.

RULE OF LAW:

Under the rule of law, lawlessness is the rule.

RULES:

1. The fewer rules you have, the fewer rules have you.
2. Rules are for fools. When people can't create, they make rules instead and when they make rules, they find it harder to create. There should be fewer rules. Obeying them is another matter: If they make sense, obey them; if they don't, ignore them. Generally, if you ignore them, they ignore you. Too many people are too scrupulous about obeying too many rules that make too little sense.
3. The rule to follow: Don't follow the rules.
4. Rules are important because they make you feel important when you ignore them.

RULES OF THE GAME:

I've always played the game though the rules are rigged, the prizes worthless, and the price too high. Fortunately, I have been lucky enough to avoid success. If you consider this sour grapes, sobeit. It happens that I like sour wine best.

RUMORS:

1. Rumors are the mother's milk of the stock market: No rumor, no sale.
2. If you want to avoid being the subject of rumors, try necrosis.
3. Whether a rumor is true or not is less important than whether or not it is believed...and belief has never had much to do with truth.
4. If you're thin, you're rumored to be suffering from AIDS or anorexia; if you're fat, you're said to deserve either AIDS or anorexia.

RUSH LIMBAUGH:

Rash lamebrain.

S

S & P INDEX:

Tho she wore a dapper diaper
'Twas hardly fun to wipe her
So, years before their ABCs
Babes must learn to S and Pee
Daintily.

SACRED:

What is sacred is the concept that nothing is sacred.

SACRIFICE:

1. A dubious notion. Do people sacrifice themselves or realize themselves through sacrifice? The devotees of the religion of sacrifice usually think more of killing than of being killed. They seem to believe they can purchase their right to the former by their readiness for the latter.
2. "We can't afford it," is the stock answer given by the Haves to the Have-nots. Strange that we never seem able to afford for the poor what we can afford for the rich. Of course, when the latter get the good things, they're not called welfare checks but development aid, investments, loans, etc. The deficit is not a condition but a disposition; we are dealing less with a state of not-having than of not-willing.
3. If you give up a lot, it will then be easier to give up a little. The reverse is not true.

Sacred

SADDAM HUSSEIN:

Likes to play thug of war.

SAFE SEX:

1. Methods to ensure that sex is boring.
2. If you enjoy oral sex, avoid buck-toothed partners.

SAINTHOOD:

1. If you can't be a hunk, be a monk.
2. A saint is someone who never sold anything she hadn't bought herself.
3. Nowadays, you have to be a saint just to be decent - the times are so rotten, the pressures so great, the values so spurious, the inducements so many, and the temptations so overwhelming.

SALEABILITY:

The less useful the product, the more likely it is to sell.

SALESMANSHIP:

1. A great salesman can sell ice to the Eskimos.
2. Technology changes; salesmanship doesn't. No matter the product, it is still sold the old fashioned way, by using guile, inculcating fear and hope, and playing on credulity.

SALVATION:

To be saved is to be miserable forever.

SALVATION ARMY:

1. Aspirin, Anacin, Acetaminophen, and Advil.
2. Trombone theology; percussion piety

SALVATION THROUGH ALTERNATION:

Some people use work to get away from their families and their families to get away from work.

SARCASM:

A stinging weapon whose victims seldom die.

SAUNAS:

Took the schvitz out of Auschwitz.

SCANDAL:

Used to be a rare treat - the dessert of politics, as it were. Today, it is the appetizer, entre, late night snack, coffee break, happy hour, breakfast, lunch and dinner. Scandal and smear are virtually all there is to politics.

SCARCITY:

Has become entirely too scarce of late.

SCEPTIC:

A member of the Permanent Opposition.

SCEPTICISM:

1. The sceptic unsceptical about his scepticism is no sceptic.
2. The fact that scepticism is self-invalidating doesn't invalidate scepticism, it confirms it.

SCHERERAZADE:

She told stories to keep alive. This is every writer's real reason for writing.

SCHIZOPHRENIA:

For some it may be the cure, not the disease.

SCHOLARLY PUBLICATIONS:

Few read them, but Tenure Committees count them and waste haulers weigh them.

SCHOOL:

Where you stick your sticky kids in order to stick it to them.

SCIENTIFIC METHOD:

No one has a monopoly on the scientific method which can also become a fetish. There is no one method applied by science which unfailingly leads to scientific results.

Seamstress

SEAMSTRESS:

Life is just sew-sew for the seamstress.

SECOND CHANCE:

1. If I could live my life over again, I wouldn't bother.
2. The desire to be born again has never been strong in me. What keeps me going is the thought that it's not forever.

SECRET AMBITION:

To die in my sleep at 80.

SECRET LIFE:

People without a secret life are people without a life.

THE SECRET OF HAPPINESS:

1. Live quietly and without hope.
2. The secret of happiness is to live each moment as though it were the first.

SECRETS:

Nothing else is worth telling.

SECURITY:

Security is the problem not the solution.

SEEING:

"Seeing is believing." Not so. Magicians make us "see" lots of things that aren't there, and science makes us believe in lots of things we can't see.

SELF-CONFIDENCE:

A certain sign of sappiness.

SELF-CONTROL:

Letting it all hang in.

SELF-ESTEEM:

1. It is said that young people today lack self-esteem. If true, they have risen in *my* estimation since they apparently realize that there is little self left to esteem.
2. Self-esteem may be based on a contempt for others.

SELF-IMPROVEMENT:

Self-improvement is all very well as long as it is you who are being improved and not the self that others want you to be.

SELFISH:

It has lately been discovered that there is a "selfish gene," which explains the bad behavior of the species. The problem with this explanation is that it doesn't explain the opposite kind of behavior, or is there an unselfish gene as well? What is not explained genetically these days? Of course, genes *may* have something to do with basic personality *structure* (whatever *that* is), but it is a very long stretch from that to concrete human *behavior* which must be socially conditioned.

SELFISHNESS:

Sometimes being selfish is the only good thing we can be - even if it is just to ourselves. In such cases, selfishness shouldn't be denigrated, especially if we reflect on some of our botched, and neither kindly received, nor kindly remembered attempts to help others.

SELF-LOATHING:

Usually lacking in the very people who need it most.

SELF-LOVE:

"Love thy neighbor as thyself," means: Love thyself first.

SELF-MOCKERY:

The armor one wears to fend off anticipated slights.

SELF-PITY:

If you don't pity yourself, who will?

SELF-PRESERVATION:

A self *worth* preserving does not take the principle of self-preservation too seriously.

SENSITIVITY:

As their technology becomes more sensitive, people become less sensitive.

SENTENCING:

If the severity of the thief's sentence was proportionate to the dollar value of what he stole, the white-collar criminal would spend years in jail, while the burglar would do "community service." Naturally, the opposite is the case.

SENIOR CITIZEN SONG:

> *Birds gotta swim*
> *Guys gotta pee...*
> *Specially...guys like me*
> *Can't help lovin' that pot of mine.*

SENTENTIOUS:

1. Those who take the pithy path.
2. A long word for a short phrase.

SEPARATE BUT EQUAL:

Separate but equal doesn't work in a society of unequals where separation is gradation.

SERIOUSNESS:

Be serious, but not overserious. Only the Court Jester could tell the sovereign seriously unpleasant truths.

SEVEN DEADLY SINS:

In the Middle Ages, they were Avarice, Envy, Gluttony, Lust, Pride, Sloth, and Wrath. At present, they are Poverty, Corpulence, Smoking, Being Black, On Welfare, Gay, and Getting Caught. Who says we're not making Progress?

SEX:

1. Spelled backwards it is: Xes (excess).
2. Used to be for reproduction; now it is for stress management.
3. Sex is easier to come by, but that does no more for it than McDonald's or Burger King (also easy to come by) do for gourmet dining.

SEX AND VIOLENCE:

The two leading causes of movies.

SEXUAL ADVERSITY:

He was not sexually abused as a child; but it was not for lack of trying. She was not sexually abused as a child; and always regretted it. He was not deprived as a child; he was depraved.

SEXUAL EDUCATION:

Clitteracy.

SEXUAL HARRASSMENT:

1. A welfare program for the legal profession.
2. Used to be called flirtation. Since it's hard to sue and collect for flirting, the name had to be changed.

SHAME:

The feeling that comes after success.

SHELTERS:

The church, military, jails, and insane asylums used to be last-resort shelters for the redundant. We are down to the jails and the military.

SHIT HAPPENS (Popular Bumper Sticker):

True enough. But why is it that a few people are able to sell it as fertilizer while the rest have to eat it?

SHOPPING SPREE:

Buy - a - rhea.

SHORT COURSE IN WESTERN ART HISTORY:

Greek art displayed the body; Christian art hid it; Renaissance art glorified it; Modern art replaced pubes with cubes.

SHORTISM:

Life is short; expect to come up short.

SHORTCOMINGS:

People have a pretty good sense of their own shortcomings which is probably why they prefer to discuss those of others.

SHOW:

The show must go on. No big deal, really - now that everything has become a show.

SHOW-OFFS:

Like firecrackers or noisemakers, they dazzle or stun for an instant.

SHOWTIME:

The program called "Eyewitness News" should be called "Eyewitless News."

SICK:

All you have to do to make people sick is claim that you've never been sick a day in your life.

SIGNS OF THE TIMES:

Pets have become more popular and people less popular.

SILENCE:

It's hard to hold your tongue, but it's worth learning how: Put a finger in your mouth instead of a foot.

SIMPLE SENTENCES:

Rudolf Flesch recommended keeping sentences to seventeen words or less (10). He did not believe in Flesching out ideas, but in Flusching them down (15).

SIMPLICITY:

Simplicity doesn't come simply.

SIN:

1. The preachers invented sin to give themselves work.
2. What the church denounces in others in order to practice itself.
3. Judaism and Christianity allowed God to do anything except sin. What, then, is the point of being God?
4. People don't want to be saved from sin, they just want to be saved from paying for it...but, if they must pay, they'd like a discount.
5. God keep me from sinning - after I am dead.

SIN AND VICE:

If sin and vice were state monopolies we could abolish taxes.

SINGAPORE:

The reason they say "bottoms up" in Singapore is that they caned sit down.

SINNER'S LAMENT:

Damned if I die and damned if I don't.

SISYPHUS:

He didn't get anywhere, but he did build muscle.

THE '60'S COMPARED TO THE '90'S:

Where once there was hope; now there is hype. If the '60's were the greening of America, the '90's are the groaning.

SIXTY-FIFTH BIRTHDAY PRESENT TO MYSELF:

Go with what you do if it's right for you.

SIZEISM:

1. The prejudice that short people can be overlooked.
2. It is politically correct to look over short people, but you should not overlook them. If you do, they may suffer sizemic tremors.
3. A nicely manicured little finger will get the same results as a big swinging dick.

SLAVE TRADE:

Fighting for things makes you free; getting them makes you their slave.

SLEEP:

Some individuals can't fall asleep because they're afraid they'll never wake; others consider that possibility to be a major incentive for sleeping.

SMALL EXPECTATIONS:

Never expect what is good to last or what lasts to be good. If it's good, figure every moment to be its last, and if it's bad, figure every moment to be lasting. If that doesn't stiffen your spine, nothing will.

SMOKE GETS IN YOUR EYES:

The best thing about the old movies is that you can watch the Stars smoke glamorously without suffering side-effects. Smoke at second hand is better than second-hand smoke. If I were a tobacco company executive, I'd forget entirely about advertising and subsidize endless re-runs of old movies in which the likes of Bogart and Bacall inhale and exhale languorously, lingeringly, and luxuriously. As I look over the number of old movies listed in my TV schedule, it occurs to me that the tobacco companies may already be doing this. Watching Betty Davis take a cigarette into her mouth is the next best thing to oral sex.

SOBRIETY:

Not among the Ten Commandments.

SOCIABILITY:

I like society as much as the next man. It's the people I can't stand.

SOCIAL NOTE:

"Mrs. Royal S. Crew breezed into town this week and is now a guest of the Tuchesleckers."

SOCIAL PROTEST:

Social protest is not dead. It has merely taken a different turn: It is now asocial, unsocial, antisocial. Marches have been replaced by muggings, demonstrations by demolitions, teach-ins by torchings, the Left by the Right, serious drama by melodrama.

SOCIAL SECURITY CRISIS:

Because the elderly (I am one of them) in our society are revered less they need Social Security more. Accelerated social change means that experience counts for less. Moreover, the daughters who took care of them in their dotage now live far away and/or work outside the home. Finally, people are living longer, and there are many more elderly. One solution, of course, would be to shoot them - but then what would the Medical Industrial Complex do without its customer base? Herein lies the germ of a solution to the Social Security crisis: Have the M.I.C. "contribute" 2% of its profits into the Social Security fund.

SOCIAL THEORY:

In the social sciences, the only proof is practical proof and that is practically impossible.

SOCIALISTS:

Fools are not all Socialists, but all Socialists are fools.

SOCIALIZATION:

The process whereby ever-weaker individuals are delivered over into the hands of ever-stronger organizations.

SOCIETY:

1. Society is based on lies. This may be the only truth in all of social science.
2. Prison without walls.

SOLACE:

Mea culpa "explains" and relieves. More satisfying still is blaming others and kicking ass.

SOLIDARITY:

Support your local undertaker: Drop Dead.

SOLITUDE:

In a world like this, you're either lonely or an asskisser.

SOLUTION:

The substitution of one problem for another.

SOLUTIONS:

The lighthouse doesn't see a solution either. It shines anyway so that others can see what to avoid.

SORRY ABOUT THAT:

People feel good about themselves when they can feel sorry for you.

SOUND BITE:

The sound gets better; the music gets worse. I'd trade the entire world music industry and its state of the art sound technology for one Vivaldi.

SOVEREIGNTY:

Sovereigns aren't expected to give up their thrones. If your job allows you sovereignty, don't be eager to give it up.

SPACE-SAVING:

I have nothing against lawns, cemeteries, or golf courses except that they take up so much valuable space. Couldn't we combine them somehow - putting the corpses under the courses, among the copses and the gorses?

SPEAKER OF THE HOUSE:

People who speak very much, fast, loud, and close rarely have anything to say and usually smell bad.

SPEAKING FRANKLY:

Speaking frankly, I never believe those who begin a sentence with, "Let me be frank," or "Speaking frankly..." Nowhere is the franking privilege more abused, of course, than in the legislature.

SPECULATION:

Too much money chasing too few people.

SPEED:

Just because we can travel faster doesn't mean we're any more successful in getting away from ourselves.

SPELLING:

Why can't people spell? What kind of education do they recieve?

SPERMBANK:

Wanker's Trust.

SPINOZA:

The Wondering Jew.

SPIRITUALISM:

1. The belief that the spirit survives the body and can be communicated with. Born in America in the 1840's, it was later taken up in Europe and has waxed and waned in popularity ever since. Since many people can't accept the idea of death, spiritualism will survive even though the spirit doesn't.
2. Spiritualism flourishes in spiritless times.

SPOKESPERSONS:

Marionettes who speak.

STABILITY:

In the Catholic and Morman churches, the old occupy all the leading positions which is why these denominations are comparatively stable. If you want stability, try gerontocracy.

STATE OF MIND:

We are awash in information, not ideas. Unfortunately, you need ideas more than you need information in order to think.

STATISTICS:

1. The numbers racket as practiced by Ph.D.'s.
2. In a democracy everyone is entitled to his own statistics.
3. If there's a will there's a way - you can prove anything with statistics.

STATUS QUO:

Voters curse the status quo all year long, but vote for it on Election Day. Apparently, the only thing worse than the status quo is change...or, perhaps, they prefer what they hate to what they fear.

STILL WATERS RUN DEEP:

George Washington kept a still on his farm.

STINGY:

Primitive people are not stingy, nor are the poor. You have to be rich to be stingy, probably because you have to be stingy to be rich.

STOCKHOLDERS:

1. They owe undivided loyalty to dividends not companies.
2. They don't own companies, they bet on them.

STOICISM:

The capacity to endure pain is so widely admired because the inclination to inflict pain is so widely distributed. Keep up your spirits, but also keep up your guard.

STOICS:

Their idea was not to enjoy life but to endure it. The Hedonists believed precisely the opposite: One enjoyed life, one didn't endure it. Both were correct: You need endurance to enjoy life, and enjoyment to endure it.

STRAIGHT ARROW:

Straight lines are not natural - even space is curved. People, too, should be free to be crooked as well as straight.

STRANGE BADFELLOWS:

Mao said that freedom comes out of the barrel of a gun, and the NRA agrees.

STUDY:

Absolutely everything is said to "need further study" except the need for further study. Who will study study? Who will research research?

STUPIDITY:

1. The only lessons worth learning are the ones that cost you dearly, which is why so many people have the good sense to stay stupid.
2. Although it is sometimes advantageous to be stupid, it is often advantageous to feign stupidity.

SUBMISSION:

Submission to one wrong invites another.

SUCCESS:

1. In our time, success is everything - what you're successful at hardly matters. The successful murderer feels as good as the successful saint. Maybe better.
2. Q. What did you do with your life? A. I tried to find truth.
   Q. Did you succeed? A. I succeeded in trying.
3. Unfortunately, when you climb to the top of the ladder, you can't kick it away.
4. Success - another name for failure.

SUCCESS SECRET:

The secret of success is very simple - never admit failure.

SUCCESS STORIES:

The two outstanding, long-term organizational success stories are the Catholic Church and the Mafia. One made money from religion, the other made a religion of money.

SUFFERING:

1. Why does God allow suffering? It's a matter of survival - there are no atheists in the foxhole.
2. How a person suffers is what makes her unique.

SUICIDE:

1. Not recommended, but it's nice to have the option.
2. If it is wrong to deprive a person of her life, why is it not wrong to deprive her of her death?
3. Suicides are people in a hurry to get where they're going.

Suicide

SUICIDE PREVENTION:

1. You should live as long as possible so that you'll be dead as short as possible.
2. The best way to keep an individual from killing herself is to tell her to go ahead. Your indifference will make her hate you and that hate, translated into a desire for vengeance, is reason enough to live.
3. As part of their general education, people should be required to spend 24 hours buried in a box.

SUICIDESPEAK:

The gift of life? Where can one return it?

SUPERIORS:

Why are our superiors almost invariably our inferiors?

SUPERMARKET SIGN:

"I will fill my shopping cart letting Jesus fill my heart."

SUPERSTITION:

The religion you don't like is superstition; the superstition you do like is religion.

SUPPLICATION:

God save us from the Godly.

SUPREME COURT:

What's supreme about it? 20 years after Roe v. Wade you still can't get an abortion in most American towns, and 40 years after Brown v. Board of Education, the last thing you're likely to receive in a Black, Hispanic, or Amerindian ghetto school is an education. Appointments to the Supreme Court are claimed by some to be the most important thing a President does. If that is true, he doesn't do much of importance.

SURFING THE INTERNET:

Getting information by surfing the Internet is like drinking water from a garden hose. You got very wet, but you still walk away thirsty.

SURGICAL SURGE:

Studies show that where there are more surgeons, there is more surgery.

SURPLUS VALUE:

Wit.

SURPRISE!!:

Life is full of surprises - few of them surprising.

SURROGATE MOTHERHOOD:

Rent-A-Womb.

SURVIVAL:

1. The need to survive is almost never the true explanation for a bad deed. Nevertheless it makes for a good excuse. Inertia and convenience explain most of our sins, but sound less compelling.

2. Being able to maintain a life of sybaritic luxury is called "surviving" nowadays. It is "surviving" if the rich and powerful need never surrender the least atom of attained privilege, however fatuous. It is this adamancy of domination, along with the unceasing compulsion to enlarge already obscene privileges, which is particularly characteristic of the Thatcher-Reaganites and their heirs and epigones who continue to rule the English-speaking world.

SUSTAINABLE DEVELOPMENT:

Either this is a euphemism for growth or an oxymoron.

SYLLOGISM:

Animals are predators. Humans are animals. Q.E.D. Humans are predators.

SYMBIOSIS:

Churches are as dependent on sin as police are on crime.

SYSTEMATIC THINKERS:

Their problem is that they are not disorganized enough.

SYSTEMS THEORY:

1. Just because the system doesn't work is no reason to abandon it. After all, things could be worse: The system could work. Then, where would we be?
2. The essence of the system is that there is no system.

T

TABLOID JOURNALISM:

1. The story is not supposed to fit the facts, the facts are supposed to fit the story and if they don't so much the worse for the facts.

> *Do not sneeze*
> *At journalese*
> *The news may not be true*
> *Who cares? - At least it's new.*

TALK:

When someone says, "We have to talk," you can be sure that they are about to tell you something unpleasant. I usually respond, "*You* have to talk, but I don't have to listen so please make sure that what you say doesn't force me to leave." Talk these days seems to swing from insult to platitude with little in between. People descry the loss of reading and writing skills, but if they would listen to themselves they'd be even more concerned with the loss of conversation, which is, after all, the basis of communication. The basic loss, of course, is what Szasz calls "self-conversation" - thinking.

TALK SHOWS:

1. Any schmuck can be a talk show host - and is.
2. Talk is cheap, which is why talk shows are ubiquitous.
3. In the case of "Crossfire" and "The McLaughlin Report," they should be called "Shout Shows..."

TALKING HEADS:

1. The country's biggest mouths and smallest minds.
2. Why is it that those with the least to say have the most to say?

TALL PEOPLE AND FAT PEOPLE:

Both get more attention because there is more of them to pay attention to, but whether that attention is favorable or unfavorable is a matter of history and geography.

TALL TALES:

Truth may be stranger than fiction, but fiction is stronger than truth: A good story lasts longer than the real story.

TASK:

Our task is not done as long as there are people who still think positively.

TASTE:

The taste of the time is established by the market, not by aesthetics. The artist's hand is less important than the invisible hand.

TASTE TEST:

As between Pepsi and Coke, I choose beer.

TAX:

For libertarians, this three letter word is a four letter word.

TAX CODE:

1. Aptly named - crack the code and you pay no tax.
2. A finely tuned instrument for enriching those who need no reward.

TAX LOOPHOLES:

A thousand points of loot.

TAX REFORM:

Every few years a couple of old loopholes are closed and a couple of new ones opened.

TAXES:

What the middle-class complains about but pays, the upper class complains about but avoids, and the lower class wishes it could complain about.

TAXING TRUTH:

Politicians don't work for the people; the people work for politicians.

TEACHING PROFESSION:

There are three million teachers in the U.S., 2,999,000 of whom are badly in need of an education.

TB (The Return of):

Diseases are like weeds: Just as soon as you think you've gotten rid of them, they come back.

TECHNOLOGY:

The cure has become the disease: Who will save us from labor-saving devices which have turned us into machine-serving dunces?

TECHNOTOPIA:

Things become human, and humans become things.

TEE VEE:

The best thing on American television is British television.

TEENAGE PREGNANCY:

We should consider paying teenagers to adopt children rather than supporting them when they have children. Alternatively, since the Catholic and Fundamentalist churches have made both birth control and abortion difficult to obtain, I'd make these churches pay for the upkeep of illegitimate children. God knows they have enough untaxed wealth. Why shouldn't the churches pay for people they are responsible for? Instead, although they are responsible for policies that cause the rest of us to pay increased taxes, they pay none.

TEETOTALER:

I never met a teetotaler yet who didn't totally tee me off.

TELEPHONE:

It was a great thing when Bell invented the telephone. It would have been an even greater thing if he hadn't.

TELEPHONE CALLS:

Sins against solitude.

TELEVANGELISM:

Salvation through donation.

TELEVASION:

Press conference.

TELEVISION:

1. The Inquisition tortured heretics; television makes them impossible.
2. The worst catastrophe that has ever happened to the human mind.
3. The beginning of the end of literacy.
4. "A vast wasteland" - still the best three-word characterization.
5. People who were once tongue-tied are now tube-tied. No matter. Before TV, they couldn't make conversation; now they don't have to. TV is the perfect diversion for the mindless: It leaves your hands free and your head empty.

TELEVISION OWNER:

Mediacracy mediocrity.

TEMPTATION:

The only way I can put myself out of the reach of temptation is to put temptation out of my reach.

Temptation

TENURE:

When you own your job.

TERM LIMITS:

1. There are three kinds of politicians: The abominable, the reprehensible, and the objectionable. Term limits are designed to provide us with a fourth kind: The perishable.
2. Term limits for legislators won't do it - the system needs term limits. Jefferson had it right: A political revolution is required every 20 years.

TERMINALS:

The termination of conversation.

TERRORIST:

1. Successful terrorists are called statesmen; unsuccessful statesmen are called terrorists.
2. Terrorists don't injure authority; they create sympathy for it.

TESTEING TIME:

Turn your head and cough.

TEXAS CHRISTIAN:

Because he believed in love so much, David Koresh made love to every young novice he could LAY his hands on.

THANKEULOGISTS:

People who send "thank you" notes for everything.

THATCHER, MARGARET:

The daughter of a grocer, only grosser.

THATCHERISM:

Mad cow disease.

THEATER OF THE ABSURD:

Waiting for Perot.

THEFT:

Massive inequality invites theft because massive inequality is theft.

THEME PARKS:

Genuine imitation fakes.

THEOLOGIAN'S TASK:

Theologians think that questions without answers deserve answers without question.

THEORY ABOUT THEORY:

1. It's only a theory.
2. There are as many theories as there are theoreticians.
3. The history of theory is the negation of theories.

THEORY AND PRACTICE:

People admire Mother Teresa but behave like Michael Miliken.

THEORY OF EVERYTHING:

Everything is relative, but relativity isn't everything.

THEORY OF RELATIVITY:

The best thing about being rich is that other people aren't.

THEOTECHNOLOGY:

Gadgets improve, people don't, which is why technology is worshipped.

THERAPISTS:

Don't let them drive you sane.

THERAPY:

1. People go to therapists with problems, but what is life except problems?
2. Do you see a therapist because you are sick, or are you sick because you see a therapist?
3. If you don't want to be labelled as mentally ill, the best thing is not to see a therapist.

THIAMIN:

I prefer women's thighs.

THIEF:

The difference between a thief and a stock-broker is that the thief doesn't try to make you think he's doing you a favor when he robs you.

THIRD PARTIES:

Waves that break before reaching shore.

THIRD PARTY:

There's been a lot of talk about forming a Third Party. But now that Bill Clinton has become a *de facto* Republican, the question that needs to be asked is: WHEN WILL A *SECOND* PARTY BE FORMED?

THIRD WAVE:

A revolution in which nothing of importance changes.

THIRTEENTH BIRTHDAY:

You reach a certain age and you ask yourself: Is this all there is?

THIRTIETH BIRTHDAY:

You ask yourself: Is it really worth it?

THIS BOOK:

Small Bierce (very small).

TICKLING:

It's a great shame that tickling never caught on. It's a marvelous way to make people happy in a hurry.

TIME:

1. Time heals all things, but what heals time is the tomb.
2. People spend their time making money in order to spend their money wasting time.
3. Why do people say, "It's only a matter of time," when time is all there is? What else would it be a matter of? There is nothing more valuable than time. "Time is money," is another stupid saying. Money you can always get more of, while time gone is gone forever. "It's all a matter of timing," shows some appreciation of reality. Shakespeare wrote, "ripeness is all" - too soon or too late is a problem. We may not understand what time is, but we should understand that a lifetime is but a life of time.

TIME FOR A CHANGE:

The magic mantra of the out-of-work politician who has nothing to say...as though things couldn't change for the worse.

TOBACCO:

Could we enjoy safe smoking if condoms were put on cigarettes?

TOBACCO SUBSIDIES:

The efforts of mass murderers should not go unrewarded.

Tobacco

TOGETHERNESS:

It's what couples have in common that gets them quarreling.

TOLERANCE:

The ability not only to eat shit but to send a thank you note to the donor.

THE TOMB OF TIME:

Did the 17th Century peasant who lived to age 22 feel he had more time than we, who live 3-1/2 times longer? We, not he, feel harried and hurried. It certainly helped that he didn't wear a watch to constantly remind him of the time. Still, there's more to it than that. We had more time when we had less time. The acceleration tendency is to blame: Just because everything takes less time, we feel like we have less time. And as the world gets more cluttered with things, people, and places we "have to" have or see and activities we "must" do, we feel we haven't enough time. The more efficient we are, the more driven; the more time we save, the less time we have. The longer we live, the longer we want to live. Thus, the extension of longevity, allegedly one of the greatest achievements of modernity, turns out not to be the key to having "enough" time. And why do we always feel we have to save time? How can you save something whose essence is transience?

TOO MUCH OF A GOOD THING:

The incidence of disease correlates directly with the incidence of doctors: The more doctors, the more disease, from which it follows: The fewer doctors, the fewer diseases. Doctors know this, which is why they tend to marry nurses, hang out with other doctors, and generally stick together. It's safer to be cynical among your own kind.

TOOL:

The fact that a tool can be misused does not make it a useless tool. What tool can't be misused? You drink water if you're thirsty and drown in it if stupid.

TOOLS OF TOOLS:

People invent tools to serve them and end up serving the tools they invented.

TORN JEANS:

"I see thy vanity through the rent in thy garment," said Socrates to the Cynic who claimed not to care about his appearance.

TOURIST:

If you haven't been in a place long enough to hate it at least a little, you don't really know it.

TRADITION:

The difference between acceptable behavior and unacceptable behavior is tradition.

TRADITIONAL CATHOLICISM:

An affinity for divinity and the trinity from here to infinity.

TRAFFIC LIGHT:

A minimum of three fatal accidents need to occur before one is put up.

TRAINING:

Not the answer to unemployment. Many of the unemployed are well-trained; others are untrained. What both groups need is work. The answer to unemployment is not more training, but more jobs - *on* which they may be trained or re-trained.

TRANSCENDENCE:

The only way to transcend the present is by realizing it.

TRANSITION:

1. This is the period we are *now* in. This is the period we are *always* in.
2. "We are living in a period of transition." Unfortunately, even the transition is a transition - perhaps to extinction.

TRAVEL:

1. More fun to recall than do.
2. Travel is all very well, but after awhile one yearns to wipe one's behind with one's favorite brand of toilet paper.

TRAVEL NOTES:

It's easier to find a needle in a haystack than a public toilet in New York City.

TRAVELLER IN TIME:

Since every *place* you travel to is crowded, you may prefer travelling in time. If you do, I recommend a visit to the very early hours of the morning. It is remarkable how little there is to bother you from 3 to 6 A.M.

TREEDOM NOW:

To save the trees, we will probably have to start living in them again.

TRIAGE:

Whatever the protocols say, rest assured that a seven figure income will put you at the front of the line. It's not Jesus who Saves, it's Mammon.

TRICKLE-DOWN ECONOMICS:

The capitalist version of socialism.

TROTSKYITES:

The Religious Left.

THE TROUBLE:

The trouble is that nothing is inaccessible any more. In a word, the trouble is that nothing is too much trouble: Everything can be done, and, therefore, is done and thus, we are undone. Obstacles have become "opportunities." "No problem" equals "big problem;" i.e., a lack of limits.

TRUE AND FALSE:

The true makes itself known via the false.

THE TRUE BELIEVER:

For the True Believer, belief does not depend on evidence, evidence depends on belief: "Evidence" that sustains belief is believed; evidence that challenges belief is not. It is a waste of time arguing with a True Believer. Argument will not change his mind; only drastically changed circumstances of the most personal, practical, and urgent kind can *possibly* do that.

TRUE CONFESSIONS:

I confess that I mind less when bad things happen to good people than when good things happen to bad people.

TRUTH:

1. Truth is not all there is to reality and it is reality we inhabit, not truth.
2. Scientists no longer search for truth. They search for grants.
3. It is said that, "The truth shall make you free." It's more apt to make you crazy.
4. Generally speaking, people who set great store on telling the truth to others, don't tell it to themselves and wouldn't know it if they saw it.
5. Uncomfortable or inconvenient truths "just need a little work."
6. Truth be told, trying to learn the truth is fine, but learning to live without it is easier.

TRUTH AND TOLERANCE:

We tolerate untruth better than truth - since it is untruth that eases our way through life and truth that tends to make things difficult. Of course, when *we* say it, we don't call it a lie, we call it "being nice," "being polite," or "protecting people's feelings."

TRUTH IN LENDING:

When you borrow money, you borrow trouble.

TRUTHS:

Errors that haven't yet been refuted.

TURBULENCE:

Look at a weather map - the normal state of the earth is turbulent.

TV NEWS:

1. Where information is entertainment and entertainment is information.
2. Seeing is disbelieving.
3. The news is made depressing in order to make the commercials look good.

TV RE-RUNS:

Enough to make Lucille Bawl.

THE TWENTIETH-CENTURY:

I suppose it's too late to return it.

TWENTIETH-CENTURY (Post World War II) CLASSICAL MUSIC:

Neither classical nor music; a colossal bore.

TWENTIETH-CENTURY PAINTING:

Daubs, dabs, and duds.

TWENTY CENTS:

A paradigm, a paradigm, a most ingenious paradigm.

20th Century Classical Music

20/20:

The most superb vision in the world won't enable you to see yourself.

21ST-CENTURY ISSUES:

Nature is becoming superfluous since we can now replicate most of it and are working on synthesizing the rest. Humanity is in the process of becoming superfluous - people are now replaceable by machines and so are people parts. Still, the number of persons increases even as the "need" for them decreases. If we remain unable to do anything about this contradiction, the job will be turned over to the machines. Unlike people, they are not bound by laws, traditions, or feelings, so we'd better be careful.

TWIGGY:

For those who fancy fornicating with skeletons.

TWILIGHT:

At night we chase a dream; during the day we chase a mirage. What, then, is the difference between sleeping and waking?

TWO CULTURES:

The wired think the unwired wintry, withered, and worm-eaten; the unwired think the wired weird, wild, and whimsical.

THE TWO PARTY SYSTEM:

1. There is only one party in America - the money party.
2. The only thing that divides the Democratic from the Republican party is the question of how to divide the spoils.

TYRANNY:

Tyranny comes to an end when the destitution that sustained it is abolished. On the other hand, there is Singapore.

Tyranny

U

ULTIMATE QUESTIONS:

1. Did Frank and Nancy make Love in the Afternoon?
2. Do Arkansas State Troopers earn overtime when they pimp for governors?
3. What would Doris Day say?

ULTIMATE REALITY:

The ultimate reality is that there is no ultimate reality. The "other" ultimate reality is that we never cease seeking the ultimate reality. Think of physics: The Greeks thought the atom was ultimate; then molecules were considered to be the last (or the least) word. Lo and behold, protons and neutrons were discovered, and now mesons and quarks are postulated. Even if this were an exercise in futility, which it is not, exercise is good for you and futility keeps your pretensions in check.

THE ULTIMATE SALESMAN:

To be able to promise everything without having to deliver anything is the unique advantage of the priest. Salesmen of the secular are handicapped by the pedestrian necessity of having to hand over a tangible product, however flawed, in return for hard cash.

UNBELIEF:

None are as likely to believe too little as those who began by believing too much.

UNCERTAINTY PRINCIPLE:

I don't expect to ever know what I want. But maybe that's not so bad. If I knew what I wanted, I might actually get it - and then what would there be left to want? Uncertainty makes things more interesting, ambiguous and spontaneous. Anyway, I'm not trying to "find myself," I'm trying to lose myself.

UNDERSTANDING:

To say that one understands nothing is to show understanding.

UNEMPLOYED:

What most employed people are, most of the time, even if they have jobs.

UNEMPLOYMENT:

1. President Coolidge brightly observed that when many people are out of work unemployment is the result. Unemployment is universally regarded as a misfortune. But doesn't it depend on what the unemployed were working at? Millions work at making other millions miserable or at robbing them blind. How bad can it be if leeches are unemployed? Isn't the question *always*: Bad for whom? Unemployment is bad, but considering what great numbers of people are unemployed at, employment may be worse.
2. The stockmarket is more fearful of inflation than unemployment. If you want to reduce the latter, dividends and capital gains should be taxed to pay for unemployment insurance.

UNEMPLOYMENT RELIEF:

While I am concerned about the plight of the unemployed, I can't help thinking of the incredible opportunities out there for con men, bunko artists, snake oil salesmen, Avon ladies, consultants, counselors, advisers, healers, therapists, used car salespersons, politicians, stockbrokers, etc. This is America, after all!...Land of opportunity...besides, it's no longer true that there's a sucker born every minute - every second is more like it...

UNEVENHANDED:

A pacifism which "equally" condemns the violence of the aggressor and the violence of the defender is morally bankrupt.

UNFLATTERING TRUTH:

The problem with flattery is that after a while people come to believe and expect it. That's how the lie was born: It all came of trying to be nice.

UNHAPPINESS:

If you've really made up your mind to be unhappy, the very best way to go about it is to singlemindedly seek happiness.

UNIONS:

Made the proletariat middle class, and since the middle class has little use for unions, it can be said that what undid the unions were the unions.

UNISEX:

The quintessential modern man is modern woman.

U.N. PEACEKEEPERS:

Their function is to keep the peace - outside the war zone. In a word, their function is containment, not peace.

U.S. CONGRESS:

Sometimes called The House of Reprehensibles.

THE U.S. SENATE:

1. Where democracy becomes gerontocracy. Although the Old Men are now being joined by Old Women, the chances are excellent that they will continue to provide us with the Old Shit. Boys will be boys, even if they are girls. The ladies are forever talking about networking, but the oldest and strongest network in the world remains the Old Boy Network.

2. The Roman Emperor Caligula made his horse a Senator. Since the U.S. Senate is already loaded with jackasses, it's good that they finally let some mares in. The offspring of their union - mules - could be useful during fillybusters.

UNIVERSITY:

The Publish or Perish universities are bad enough, but the publish perish the thought universities are even worse.

UNITY:

The temporary amalgamation of the permanently divided.

Unity

UNKIND REFLECTIONS AT THE BIRTHDAY PARTY OF A 90 YEAR OLD, BY HIS HEIR PRESUMPTIVE:

"There is such a thing as over-staying one's welcome."

UNPLEASANT TRUTH:

The truth is like medicine. It tastes lousy, but it's good for you.

UNPLEASANTNESS:

It's extremely unpleasant being right when everyone else is wrong.

UNPROTECTED SEX:

Come as you are.

UPWARD MOBILITY:

Some boys grow up wanting to be President. But if you are truly ambitious, there is only one goal worth striving for: The Papacy. What it must feel like to be *Infallible!*

URINARY RETENTION:

1. Prostate with grief.
2. Inability to "go with the flow."
3. Men-o-pause.

USEFUL AND USELESS (The Difference):

Useful: What we know we need.
Useless: What we don't know we need.

USEFUL INVENTIONS OR INVENTING USES:

Inventions can be useful, but the invention of uses for inventions can be just as useful. Invention is the mother of use, but sometimes she doesn't get pregnant quickly.

UTAH:

Where people are too uncivilized to be immoral.

UTILITARIANISM:

We tolerate easily in the rich and useless what we condemn vigorously in the poor and useful. Thus, a Rupert Murdoch is welcomed with open arms to the U.S. (We do so very much NEED his learned contributions to our cultural life!) while a poor peasant from Mexico has to sneak in, at great risk for the privilege of toiling in sub-human conditions to plant and harvest the food we eat.

UTOPIA:

1. Imagine a life without loneliness. . .one that is not empty. That is just what we have: Clutter, crowds and noise.
2. The best synonym for utopia is myopia.

V

VACATION:

1. A temporary truce with life.
2. The most exhausting experience you can imagine. If you need a rest, go back to work.

VALENTINE'S DAY:

Love and Kitsches.

VALUE:

1. Things don't cost what they're worth, they're worth what they cost.
2. The value of a thing only becomes clear when we are deprived of it.

VALUE OF A COLLEGE EDUCATION:

The value of a college education is trivial compared to the value of getting young people out of the house.

VALUE OF EDUCATION:

Anyone can be a fool, but to be a learned fool, you have to go to school.

VANITY:

1. When you're surrounded by pygmies, it's easy to think yourself a giant.
2. To deny one's vanity is to confirm it.

Vanity

VANITY PRESS:

Highly recommended for those who want their work published, but don't care if it's read.

VARIETY:

Variety is not the spice of life; it is its essence. Spice merely enhances flavor, but variety is flavor.

VATICINATING IN THE VATICAN:

Now that the paintings in the Vatican have been cleaned, it is clear that if Michelangelo were alive today he would be a cartoonist.

VEGETARIAN:

1. One who feels that a life without fruit is a fruitless life.
2. With vegetarians, you don't only break bread, you break wind. Although they're not usually members of the Far Right, their diet forces them to fart right - and they're very fartright about it, too.

VEGETARIANISM:

Plants don't kill people; people do. The ethical alternative is Cannibalism.

VICE:

1. An excess of virtue is the worst vice.
2. Ban vice and you raise its price. Higher prices attract The Mob, turning what were once cottage industries into industrial strength Evil Empires.
3. Prohibition doesn't diminish sin, it increases its attractiveness: Forbidden fruit always tastes better.
4. Few things go further toward making life tolerable.

VICTIM:

I have a natural sympathy for the victim but a natural antipathy to becoming one.

VICTIMOLOGY:

Given the current explosion of victim's rights, if you're not a victim, you'll soon become one.

VICTORIA'S SECRET:

Spousal arousal.

VICTORY:

Victories come and go. Defeats have a lasting effect.

VIEW FROM THE TOP:

Dissolve the people - and elect another.

VILLAINY:

Great Villains exert a fascination all their own. Why? Villainy is an art form requiring theatricality, nerves of steel, imagination, and a wholesome distaste for good, honest work. Since we envy the villain his talents and share some of his resentment toward the established order, we are grateful to him for acting out our feelings and providing us with vicarious, riskless thrills.

VINDICATION:

The four sweetest words in the language: I told you so.

VIRTUAL REALITY:

1. When the material becomes meta-real.
2. When I grew up "accept no substitute" was a key advertising slogan. Today, everyone crows about virtual reality substitution, par excellence. Everything is ersatz, synthetic, pre-fabricated, pre-digested, and eviserated. How could it be otherwise? We have so exploited and mined nature that it is no longer cheap and easy to make much money from squeezing her. Substitutes have to be invented to keep the wheels of commerce turning.

VIRTUE:

Virtue is its own punishment; vice its own reward.

VISIONARY:

Someone lacking a clear goal.

VIVE LA DIFFERENCE:

Women can get pregnant which is why they're more hopeful about the future.

VOIDS, JUST VOIDS:

Nowadays you can be anything, but you can't just be; you can do anything, but you can't do nothing; you can go anywhere, but you have to have a goal; you can walk, but it better be to somewhere; you can say anything, but it has to have a point. A void to the wise is sufficient; a void to the fool, isn't.

VOLTAIRE:

He ridiculed Leibniz for the unthinking optimism of, "It's all for the best in the best of all possible worlds." Voltaire got it wrong. Those words are not a statement of optimism but resignation. Read them again.

VOLUNTARY POVERTY:

Doesn't help the poor or hurt the rich.

VOLUNTEERS:

It's hard to supervise people who are doing you a favor.

W

THE WAGES OF SIN:

From Fatal Attraction to fetal contraction.

WAITING GAME:

When the only game in town is rigged, you can participate or stand aside - or so it seems. If you participate, you're knowingly engaging in fraud; if you stand aside, you're criticized for letting things go to hell. So, what do you do? You neither participate or stand aside. You watch, you criticize privately and, if possible, publicly, and you wait. And when the situation ripens and a proper moment arrives, you try to act properly. But, what if it never arrives? "Never" is too long to predict. Although it may not arrive in your lifetime, it might in the lifetime of the people you help to understand or the people they, in turn, help to understand. The system isn't seamless and sooner or later cracks will appear that either you or your heirs can help widen. Dissenters are a community in time as well as space.

WAKE-UP CALL:

A signal to switch from one fantasy (or nightmare) to another.

WALKING:

The best exercise for the mind, if not for the body, hence peripatetic philosophy. If you're lucky enough to have someone to talk with when you walk, wonderful; if not, talk to yourself; i.e., think.

WANTS:

The problem is not that we can't get what we want, it is that what we get isn't worth much.

WAR:

1. Look at the bright side - too many people live too long. Sure, it's always the "wrong people" who get killed, but nothing's perfect, is it?
2. The word "war" is now obsolete having been replaced with the phrase "peace process."

WARFAIR:

No one has time any more for nice, serious, long, luxurious, warm wars, so we have to rest content with weekend wars, quickies, in[and out]vasions, evasions, poll-prodding pugilistics, and made-for-TV tiffs. Besides providing promotional possibilities for the officer caste and pre-election promos for presidential pretenders, these gala affairs keep the military-industrial complex busy and able to test in real time the latest in liquidation and the extremes in extermination weapons before selling or giving them to Turd World dictators.

WASHOUT:

Pilate asked "What is Truth?" and turned away to wash his hands without waiting for an answer. He wasn't the last one to wash his hands of Truth.

WEALTH:

What you are makes you independent; what you have makes you dependent.

WEATHER:

1. Never right.
2. Should be spelled "whether" - since we never know whether to believe it.

WEATHER CHANNEL:

The only reason they get away with their lousy long-range predictions is that we have short-range memories.

WELFARE BUDGET:

When the welfare budget decreases, the police budget increases.

WELFARE CHECK:

The money we pay the poor so that we can abuse, feel superior to, and blame them for everything. Given how little they get from us compared to how much shit they have to take from us, they're a bargain.

WELFARE REDUCTION AS A WAY TO CUT PREGNANCIES:

Starvation has never been an effective birth control device - look at the places in the world where there is famine and note how populous they are. Misery makes babies.

WELL-ADJUSTED:

Well-adjusted people are just maladjusted people who take their medicine without making a face, believe everything they're told, and accept the unacceptable. Well-adjusted people are sick.

WELLNESS:

Wellness sells because illness thrives.

WHAT HAPPENS WHEN YOU O.D. ON COFFEE:

Folger's in your kupf.

WHAT IS TO BE DONE?:

Reason is needed to heal the wounds inflicted by reason.

WHAT IS TRUTH?:

1. Good question.
2. Anything defensible.

WHAT'S IN A NAME?:

1. Plenty. If the first men who walked on the moon had been properly named, hundreds of billions of dollars might have been saved. Instead of calling them astronauts, we should have called them astronuts or lunatics.
2. Not much. Abraham Lincoln and Richard Nixon were both called Republicans.

WHEN NASA HAD ITS ASSA IN A NOOSA:

All the hubbub when the Hubble bubble burst.

WHIGGISH:

One who prefers piggish to priggish.

WHINING:

I prefer lack of communication to communication of lack.

THE WHITE HOUSE:

A smoke-free environment - not a smoke-and-mirrors-free environment.

THE WHITE HOUSE PRESS CORPS:

They cover the stories, but first they cover their asses.

WHITE MAN'S BURDEN:

All that he was able to plunder from the black, brown, red, and yellow man.

WHITEWATER:

First it was Bill; then it was Hillary. Can Chelsea be far behind?...and there is still the potentially pestiferous problem of whether Socks made water in Whitewater...

WHITHER WITHER?:

Communism predicted the state would wither away. Instead, Communism withered away. The mistake Lenin made was to think that because government couldn't solve problems it would disappear - when, in fact, that very inability constituted the reason for its continuance: Government exists not to solve problems but because problems are insoluble.

WHY:

When the question is "Why?" the answer is money.

WHY PEOPLE GO TO QUACKS:

More pain makes less sane.

WILDERNESS:

Unmarketed nature.

WILDLIFE MANAGEMENT:

The wildlife that needs to be managed is not four- legged but two-legged.

WISDOM:

1. In some societies, the old are considered useless, in others, wise. In fact, there is no contradiction. The wise have long since discovered

the folly of utility. After all, the useless don't have to do anything, the useful do it all for them.
2. When you're young you'd better be smart; when you're old you'd better be pleasant.

WOMEN:

1. "What do women want?" asked Freud, plaintively. What the hell did he think they want? The same as men want. But that didn't become obvious 'till recently. What women want is money, power, attention, and to be worshipped, adored, and obeyed. Whom do you suppose they learned all that from? Right: Men. And whom do you suppose men learned it from: Their mothers. What goes around, comes around. The differences between the sexes are anatomical; the similarities are sociological, and the rest is comical.
2. Some women like losers. For them, there's nothing more winning than losing since it makes them feel superior.

WOMEN'S LIB:

A clever scheme devised by men who were liberated from labor by it, while women were liberated to labor through it. Both got what they wanted - what the other had. But guess who got the better deal, as usual?

WORK:

It is said that you should not mix work and play. If we didn't, we'd be playing all the time.

WORKAHOLIC:

Liking your alcohol doesn't make you an alcoholic and liking your work doesn't make you a workaholic.

WORKING HYPOTHESIS:

Men and women who enjoy what they do and don't work too hard, by and large, get more pay than those who hate what they do and are bored and exhausted doing it. Justice would be served by exactly the opposite set of rewards and punishments, but compensation has little to do with justice and much to do with power in the economically determined society.

WORLD TRAVEL:

Has become both easier and more tedious, more convenient and less enjoyable, cheaper and more expensive; trips are quicker, planning and recovery slower. If you think too much before you travel, you won't. If you travel before you think too much, you will. Do me just one favor if you do go: Think about it *after* you return. Don't just tell me it was "great."

WORRIES:

1. The best way to stop worrying about one problem is to find another one to worry about. You don't solve problems, you exchange them.
2. If you can still worry, there's nothing to worry about. It's when you can't worry that you need to worry.

WORTH:

Are Michael Jackson and Michael Eisner worth 200 million dollars a year? You don't get what you're worth, you're worth what you get.

WRINKLES:

Caused by excessive exposure to the sun. If you love sun-bathing but can't stand wrinkles, cover your face and bare your bottom. Tans are big in Cannes - especially if they're big cans.

WRITER:

A writer on the wagon is like a fish out of water.

WRITER TO READER:

"Let each one gather from this work the fruits that he can, according to the capacity of his bowl; because there is nothing so wicked that it may not be converted to the profit and usefulness of good people; and there is nothing so good and worthy that it cannot be the cause and material of scandals of bad people." Giordano Bruno, philosopher, poet, dramatist, and martyr in the cause of intellectual freedom.

WRITERS AND PUBLISHERS:

Those who write books have ever been in thrall to those that keep them.

WRITING:

1. I write because I have to - what other reason is there?
2. The ultimate game of Solitare.
3. A serious writer finds writing harder than other people.
4. Writing to live is one thing; living to write, another.

Writing

WRITING A DAILY COLUMN:

When writing becomes a rite it feels wrong.

WRITING APHORISMS:

It beats doing crossword puzzles. Those of us who are addicted may be said to be sentenced to the sententious.

WRITING PROFESSIONALLY:

I don't get paid for exercising my body; why should I get paid for exercising my mind? If you regard your writing as a kind of diary, who cares if it gets published?

WRONG IS RIGHT:

Allowing people to be wrong is usually right...more right than over-prescribing rules by which they must live in order always to be right. To be right in every particular is to be wrong in general - and in the long run, which is coming shortly.

X

XANTIPPE:

Socrates' wife, the most famous shrew in history. Tradition tells us she enjoyed making him miserable and, in response, he enjoyed the favors of men and boys. Whether this is true or whether she made him miserable because he was messing around, we will never know, anymore than we will ever know whether he spent his time as he did trying to avoid her tongue or find theirs. Still, they were said to be devoted to one another, and he claimed she taught him patience. We will also never know whether she, too, found consolation elsewhere - the *National Enquirer* not yet having begun publication. One shrewd shrew, Xantippe did it her way: She achieved immortality not because she was his wife, but because he was her husband.

Y

YAWN:

The half-suppressed yawn makes a louder statement than the most sarcastic remark.

YELLOW JOURNALISM:

As distinguished from the other kind which is now extinct.

YOUNG AND OLD:

Young people think old people are fools, but old people know young people are fools.

YOUNG IN HEART:

"You're as young as you feel," said the oldster. Yes, and we know how quickly feelings pass and how long facts last. The most pathetic thing about old age in The New Age is that it doesn't want to grow up and can't accept growing old. It wants to stay young and foolish forever, but only the latter is possible.

YOUR FUNERAL:

Probably the only stage production in which you will ever star.

YOUTH CULTURE:

When I was growing up kids tried to look and act like adults; now, adults try to look and act like kids.

Z

ZAFTIK:

A Yiddish word meaning pleasantly plump. Much used in the '30's, as a compliment to women. Shows how times have changed. The only thing worse now (in the Age of Thin when assertiveness is in) than being plump is being pleasant. Soft and chubby are out, lean and mean are in. Missing this misplaced maternalism, men have turned to each other for comfort. Thus, we have a "men's movement" which stresses the feminine in the masculine. And all because they miss their mothers - who were Zaftik.

ZEN:

An attachment to detachment. It's not true that Zen masters have no desire - they desire to be free of desire.

ZERO SUM GAME:

Defeat of one disease makes life easier for another disease.

ZIPPER:

One of the cleverest inventions of the 20th-Century. But do make sure it's done up when you get through and don't get your you-know-what caught while you're doing it up.

Zippers are a snap
But watch for Zipper Zap.

ZOOM:

The most important political innovation of the last half of the 20th Century was the Zoom camera. 5 o'clock shadow and visible sweat cost Nixon the Presidency; looking clumsy lost it for Ford; looking indecisive for Carter; looking dumb for Bush and Quayle; looking wooden for Mondale, Dukakis, and Dole. (Watch out Gore.) Reagan and Clinton look relaxed in front of a camera. Since the invention of the Zoom, political science has become obsolete having been replaced by cosmetic science.

ZOOS:

I wouldn't object to zoos if people were caged and animals could look at them. After all, people are used to being in cages, animals aren't. The current justification for zoos is that they are safe, if boring, havens for endangered species. But it works both ways: Because there are safe havens, it becomes all too easy to justify continued killing and catching of creatures in the wild. Still, as someone growing up poor in a big city, I remember that going to the zoo made me feel liberated from the ordinary...

EPILOGUE: TO THE READER (again!)

This book is self-published. Not that I didn't try to find an agent and/or a publisher. But you know how it is these days: If you haven't murdered your wife or defended the murderer of someone else's wife or done something else outrageous (looted a bank, cut off a penis, sexually abused a centenarian, fetus or a child) - something that will catch and hold the media's increasingly fleeting attention for more than six seconds and make you an overnight sensation - until the next night - if you haven't done any of these things who cares about your book? It is of no importance, because there's no money in it. Or if you can't be a centerfold, you might as well fold up your tent.

Besides, if your idea is to tell it like it is, pulling no punches, do it your way - to trot out all the cliches - in a word, if you don't want to be censored (sometimes called "edited") or find yourself exercising self-censorship in an effort not to displease any possible asshole - the only way to do it is to do-it-yourself.

So, like I said, this book is self-published.

By the way, I am not implying that nothing good gets published commercially or by subsidized presses these days. My own estimate is (and I have followed book publishing pretty carefully for more than four decades) that about 10% of what is published is worthwhile and about 1% of what is published, pushed, and publicized is worthy. Which is one way of saying that even if your worthwhile book does get published, it will most probably have a shelf life of two to three months or, if you're lucky, three to four months before being remaindered, pulped, or shredded for kitty litter. Two or three years of effort; two or three months of life. Doesn't seem too positive a cost/benefit outcome. All in all, therefore, I thought I'd try it on my own - slowly, carefully, lovingly. If I can reach a few readers who will find something there, it will mean more than having a mass of morons embarrassing me with their canned kudos. (I've had a little experience with that, having been published in national magazines and newspapers.)

If this all sounds like sour grapes sobeit. I like sour wine.

P.S. If you liked what you read, I will send a copy to anyone else you think might enjoy this book. Simply send me their address and a check and I'll do the rest!